How Obama Governed

How Obama Governed
The Year of Crisis and Challenge
by
Earl Ofari Hutchinson

P R E S S

Printed in the United States

Published by
Middle Passage Press
5517 Secrest Drive
Los Angeles, California 90043

Designed by Alan Bell

Publisher's Cataloging-in-Publication
(Provided by Quality Books, Inc.)

Hutchinson, Earl Ofari.
    How Obama governed : the year of crisis and challenge / by Earl Ofari Hutchinson.
    p. cm.
    Includes bibliographical references and index.
    LCCN: 2009910137
    ISBN-13: 978-1-4392-5999-3
    ISBN-10: 1-4392-5999-2
1. Obama, Barack. 2. Political leadership—United States. 3. Presidents—United
States—History—21st century. 4. United States—Politics and government—
2009- 5. United States—Economic conditions—2009- 6. United States—Foreign
relations—2009-   I. Title.
E907.H88 2010   973.932
                        QBI09-600188

Table of Contents

How Obama Governed

Not
Black President Obama,
President Obama

*M*idway through his speech announcing his candidacy for the presidency at the Old Capitol Building in Springfield, Illinois on February 10, 2007 Barack Obama gave two solid clues as to how he would govern. The first clue was his flat assertion, "What's stopped us from meeting these challenges is not the absence of sound policies and sensible plans. What's stopped us is the failure of leadership, the smallness of our politics - the ease with which we're distracted by the petty and trivial, our chronic avoidance of tough decisions, our preference for scoring cheap political points instead of rolling up our sleeves and building a working consensus to tackle big problems." The other clue came in what he didn't say. He mentioned race only once and then so tangentially that it passed virtually unnoticed and for the moment uncommented on.

The moment quickly passed. After Obama announced he was a presidential candidate the twin mantra of the army of pundits, analysts, and inveterate presidential campaign watchers was that he could be the first black to be president. If that happened it would go far toward proving America had finally kicked its race syndrome. The twin mantra was repeated ad infinitum during the campaign. It was dead wrong about Obama and the presidency. He was not running as a black presidential aspirant, he was running as a presidential aspirant. He had to make the crucial distinction for personal and political purposes.

He made the point oddly enough on the *Fox News Network* which was staunchly opposed to him, "Is race still a factor in our society? Yes. I don't think anybody would deny that. Is that going to be the determining factor in a general election? No, because I'm absolutely confident that the American people—what they're looking for is somebody who can solve their problems."

The ritual preface of the word "black" in front of every achievement or breakthrough an African-American makes is insulting, condescending and minimizes their achievement. It maintains and reinforces the very racial separation that much of America claims it is trying to get past. Dumping the historic burden of race on blacks measures an individual's success or failure by a group standard. That's a terrible burden for any group to shoulder. They succeed or fail solely as individuals.

Obama's personal history—his bi-racial parents, his upbringing, his education, and his relative youth— defied racial pigeonholing. He was influenced, but not shaped, by the rigid race grounded civil rights struggles of the 1960s as older whites and blacks were. The institution of the presidency, and what it takes to win the office, demands that racial typecasting be scrapped anyway. Obama would have had no hope of bagging the presidency if there had been the slightest hint that he embraced the race tinged politics of Al Sharpton and Jesse Jackson. His campaign would have been marginalized and compartmentalized as merely the politics of racial symbolism.

He could not have raised record amounts of campaign cash. He would not have been fawned over by legions of Hollywood celebrities, corporate and union leaders. He would not have netted the endorsements of Colin Powell and packs of former Reagan and Bush Sr. administration stalwarts, and prepped by W. Bush political guru Karl Rove on how to beat Hillary Clinton. The media would never have given him the top heavy favorable coverage, endorsements, nor relentlessly hammered Republican rival John McCain. If the media had so chosen, it could have torpedoed Obama's campaign by playing up his connection with his race focused former pastor, Jeremiah Wright. It bought his protest of racial shock and bewilderment at the revelations of Wright's race baiting sermons. It dropped the matter and it never again surfaced as a serious campaign issue.

* * * * *

*O*bama had to cling closely to the centrist blueprint Bill Clinton laid out for Democrats to win elections, and to govern after he won. The second clue he gave in his Springfield speech gave ample testimony to the real politic of presidential governance if a president is to have any hope of success in the office. It means stress on bipartisanship, compromise, conciliation, and at times retreat on political aims and even principles. The best example of that is Ronald Reagan. In rhetoric and stated belief he was a doctrinaire states' rights defense hawk who as a presidential candidate railed against big government.

Once elected, he didn't change his beliefs but he understood successful statecraft required a give and take with Democratic foes. If there was enough give he could win passage of his prime legislative and policy initiatives. Presidents need these wins. Then they can spin them as major victories for their policies. Reagan was a master at that. Obama understood the same thing; that the give in political horse trading is sometimes more crucial to getting things done than the take. In a mid air talk with reporters on Air Force One en route to an economic conference in Chicago in February, 2009, Obama made his trademark pitch for bipartisanship,

"Going forward, each and every time we've got an initiative, I am going to go to both Democrats and Republicans and I'm going to say, 'Here is my best argument for why we need to do this. I want to listen to your counterarguments. If you've got better ideas, present them; we will incorporate them into any plans that we make, and we are willing to compromise on certain issues that are important to one side or the other in order to get stuff done.'"

Obama's willingness to take compromised, nuanced positions on policy issues was evident during the campaign in his shifts on health care, the death penalty, gays in the military, religious conservatism, the Foreign Intelligence Surveillance Act (FISA), abortion, the Iraq war, and the war on terrorism. This drew soft mutters from some progressives and liberal Democrats that Obama had back flipped on these issues. His transition from solid progressive positions on issues as an earlier state senator and US senatorial candidate was even more evident once in the White House. His emphasis on strong defense, the war against terrorism, a fluid plan for winding down the Iraq War, and a big troop build-up in Afghanistan, retreat from his plan for a major tax hike on the rich, a cautious plan for affordable health care and for dealing with the sub-prime lending crisis, and a genteel reproach of Wall Street brought increasingly louder grumbles of retreat, and betrayal from progressives and liberal Democrats.

A president as distinct from a presidential candidate's shifts on policy matters is only one gauge of a president's need for give and take political flexibility. There was also the old axiom that you can tell a president by his staff and cabinet picks. This very much applied to Obama. A cast of governors, senators and ex senators, former Clinton and Democratic Party operatives and even a few token Republican mavericks were floated for his staff and cabinet picks early on.

The list read like a who's who of the Beltway and Heartland American political establishment. The idea to load up his administration with familiar names was that they were the most experienced and seasoned administrators and political operatives. Picking them would avoid a power vacuum and quiet the criticisms repeatedly tossed at him during the campaign that he was too inexperienced to govern.

* * * * *

*O*bama's cautious, bi-partisan approach and his Beltway establishment staff and cabinet picks were designed to blunt the standard Republican rap that Democrats, especially one they branded a liberal Democrat, inherently pander to special interests, i.e. minorities, are pro expansive government, and anti-business, and military spending. Even though he never veered from the center his first year in office that did not stop the furious counterinsurgency from GOP operatives, conservative bloggers, talk show jocks and the *Fox News Network*. No matter what he said or did he was simply too inviting a political target not to go after with a vengeance.

An Obama White House was a historic and symbolic first. However, it was a White House that kept a firm, close to the vest and conciliatory eye on mid-American public opinion, along with corporate and defense industry interests in making policy decisions and determining priorities. All other occupants of the White House had to do the same. Obama would and could not have attained the White House if he didn't do the same. This had nothing to do with race, or the obsession of a black president, first or not. His quick move to the center had everything to do with the tailored and well-formulated requirement of White House governance.

CHAPTER 1

How Obama Governed

B arack Obama was virtually an unknown U.S. senatorial candidate from Illinois when he took the podium at the Democratic National Convention held at the Fleet Center in Boston on July 27, 2004. He delivered a 17 minute keynote talk that nearly every expert then and in the months afterward agreed made him an instant national figure. The speech also created a buzz among Democratic Party insiders that he might also be a viable presidential candidate.

The memorable line that he uttered in the speech that stuck was his challenge to the politicians to cease talk that America was hopelessly divided into blue states and red states. He declared there was just one nation. Yet almost forgotten in the post speech euphoria and backslapping was that as political speeches go it was stock stuff.

Obama didn't toss out a single new idea that politicians don't routinely proclaim—the tout of freedom, democracy, America's greatness, hope for everyone, opportunity, government serving the people, need for openness, and eschewing wars. Obama rehearsed, tinkered with, and fretted over the speech for weeks before as one advisor cautioned him "to get it right."

Mundane or not, canned or not, the speech set the tone both for a future presidential campaign, and an administration if victorious. It was moderate, conciliatory, even compromising. It played it safe on the issues. The crafting of the speech and the toil on it was a telling sign about his personal and political style and approach. He tried and tested parts of the speech on friends, staff members and informal advisors.

The speech alerted the Democratic Party leaders and corporate financial donors that the soon to be freshman US Senator from Illinois was not only a fresh face, but someone who would not make rash, hasty, ill thought out or out of the political mainstream box decisions as the party's future potential presidential nominee.

Obama's caution was on full display in the 17 minute speech. But it was really just reflective of the caution that was amply exhibited in his performance record on policy issues during his years in the Illinois state legislature. During the campaign McCain and GOP conservatives slapped him with the tag of the most liberal of the Senate Democrats. This was inaccurate and deliberately misleading. A cursory read of his record, as well as a fine comb of his speeches, statements, and interviews, showed that he never claimed bragging rights as the "most liberal Democratic senator." Even then, he was a pragmatic, centrist, Democrat who when circumstances dictated, would conciliate conservatives on an important issue, especially one that might cause him political trouble.

His voting record in the Illinois state legislature gave the strongest hint of that. He got high marks from liberal groups on votes on environmental, gun control, abortion, civil liberties protections, and ethics reform. But he also deftly ducked taking positions on some of the same issues when they could stir rancor and were potentially polarizing. "I learned that if you're willing to listen to people, it's possible to bridge a lot of the differences that dominate the national political debate," he told an interviewer in 2007, "I pretty quickly got to form relationships with Republicans, with individuals from rural parts of the state, and we had a lot in common."

He voted present (i.e. no position) on bills that would have prohibited a partial birth abortion procedure, reduced penalties for a first offense for carrying a concealed weapon, mandatory prosecution for firing a gun near school grounds, that protected the privacy of sex abuse victims, prohibited strip clubs and other adult establishments from being within 1,000 feet of schools, churches, and day care centers, and two parental notification abortion bills. Illinois legislators vote present when they are uncertain or have qualms about some points about a bill. Moderate Democrats in the Illinois legislature vote present when they have reservations about a conservative tinged law and order bill. They worry that by opposing it they will be typed as soft on crime. That would enrage conservatives. Legislators also vote present when they don't want to go on record against a bill that they oppose.

During his stint in the legislature Obama often used the "present "vote and rarely gave a reason why he abstained from voting.

Whatever his motive for not taking a firm stand on these issues, and not spelling out the reason why, it helped burnish his credentials with conservative Republicans and right leaning Democrats as a man willing to compromise even conciliate on big ticket issues that conservatives routinely support or oppose.

Obama's firm commitment to political centrism and bipartisanship was evident in his approach to picking a Supreme Court justice. The early names that were batted around were mostly former Clinton officials and judicial appointees. When it came time to actually choose a new justice, he signaled that he would consult with Senate Republicans to insure that his pick would draw no more than their obligatory verbal opposition, but that ultimately his pick would sail through.

His choice of Sonia Sotomayor to replace David Souter on the Supreme Court in May 2009 was the test. He prepped key Republicans on the Senate Judiciary Committee about Sotomayor. That worked to damp down some of the more war like rhetoric from the GOP Senators against her. "I definitely think we need to have the respectful tone and we need to look at the record," said Texas Senator Kay Bailey Hutchinson, "We need to have the responsibilities that have been put on us by the Constitution taken very seriously."

As predicted, conservatives and the GOP senators still hammered her as too liberal, and too much of a judicial activist in her legal philosophy and rulings. Privately, though, most recognized she was none of those things. Her rulings were moderate, legally sound, and squarely in the judicial mainstream. There was never any real doubt that despite the requisite GOP squawks that she wouldn't be confirmed.

She did not change the ideological dominance of conservatives on the bench. A future Obama pick just might and that would be a far better test and challenge for him and his philosophy about who should sit on the High Court and how vehement Republican opposition would be to his pick no matter how hard he worked to assuage them then Sotomayor was.

Obama's cautious baby steps on policy issues and court picks during the campaign was an open nod to conservative Republicans. Despite this, there was virtually no chance that this would soften their campaign attacks on him as too liberal, even radical, and too much of a big, intrusive government advocate. They were going to watch closely for any hint of a pander to minorities, pro choice, environmentalists, pro ACLU, and gun control advocates and any group deemed anti-business.

It was wise that he didn't claim to be the leading liberal that GOP attackers routinely smeared him as. Still, he wasn't, but that didn't ease the concern of the legion of Obama backers who read more into him and his record than was ever there. He gave the look and feel of a radical departure from Bush, and that alone brought joy—for a while. But the hard reality of White House governance wouldn't be any different for him than any other president.

* * * * *

The fear of GOP conservatives and the hope of liberals and progressives that he would govern different, though, were palpable from the first moment that he hit the campaign trail. There was the tense and riveting moment at a McCain campaign rally in Minnesota on October 28, 2008 when a flustered and livid participant shouted at McCain that he was scared of an Obama presidency. The man was hardly alone in his professed terror of an Obama White House. Even before McCain and Sarah Palin's brief mudsling at him as a socialist and radical, large numbers of McCain backers quietly grumbled that an Obama White House would be a disaster.

The fear was that he was too liberal, even radical, too young, too willing to appease foreign foes, and too much a Democratic Party shill, and for some, his race. As the prospect of an Obama White House loomed larger, the skepticism, worry, and fear of those like the fearful man at the McCain rally grew. That fear would have been there even if race and all Obama's other alleged liabilities weren't there.

Obama raised the bar high on expectations, maybe too high. He was expected to immediately deliver on his promise to clamp down on Wall Street, implement affordable health care, end the war in Iraq, and make good on his promise to cut taxes for virtually everyone while not raising taxes. With the treasury awash in debt, and the likelihood of even more debt from the projected cost of funding his health care reform plan and the stimulus package, this was the riskiest promise of all. Voters tend to remember sweeping promises that candidates make in the heat of an election battle.

There were other signs of potential danger to an Obama White House. One was the curse of a first term president who takes power from an incumbent of the opposite party. The partisan attacks, character assaults, second guessing on policy decisions, and resistance against Clinton and Bush were relentless their first months in office.

Millions of voters simply did not accept their election and gave them no grace period to find their Oval Office legs.

The inexperience tag that Hillary Clinton and McCain slapped on Obama during the campaign would be dredged up to explain any real or perceived misstep or failing by him in the White House. Obama backers parried the attack during the campaign by turning the table and proclaiming that his lack of national and especially international experience was a positive. That he'd bring fresh ideas and approaches to statecraft that replace the old, tired, and failed polices of recent times. The more exuberant turn the table again and say that his tenure on the Senate Foreign Relations Committee, the Veterans Affairs Committee, and Homeland Security, make him even more experienced than Jimmy Carter, Ronald Reagan, Bill Clinton, and Bush, when they took office. Still, the inexperience tag is a politically perilous one.

Many voters expect American presidents to hit the ground running. They are unwilling to make a leap of faith that an untested candidate can smoothly and effortlessly handle all the crisis situations that inevitably arise. The reality is that inexperienced presidents often make poor crisis managers. They have gotten the country into costly and unpopular wars and brush fire conflicts. They alienate foreign friends and allies. They bungle the economy. And their administrations more times than not are riddled with corruption and cronyism. The disastrous proof is the administration of the man that Obama replaced.

Bush's foreign and domestic policy bumbles and ineptitude didn't mean that Obama would implode under fire or be saddled with the towering political ills of Bush. Yet, his avowed political enemies made no pretense that that's exactly what they wanted to happen. Leading Obama foe Rush Limbaugh was asked in his words by "a major American print publication" to assess in 400 words what he expected of an Obama's administration. Limbaugh boasted to his radio listeners that he didn't need 400 hundred words to answer that. He could say it in four: "I hope he fails." It was blunt and brutal, and thousands more happily agreed with him.

* * * * *

*O*bama's most fervent boosters on the campaign trail namely African-Americans, liberal Democrats and progressives passionately hopped on the Obama bandwagon because they believed that he could quickly undo the damage of the Bush years. His subsequent reversal on FISA, his rejection of public financing, his tout of the death penalty for child rape, his backpedal from his pledge to sit down for talks with Iranian President Mahmoud Ahmadinejad, and his retreat to a glacially slow, vaguely laid out timetable for a phased withdrawal from Iraq drew mild gasps from some of his less fervent backers.

However, even when he shouted out at campaign rallies his promise to shake up the Washington establishment; he never made any promise to make big sweeping changes. He could not have won the presidency without engaging in the traditional deal making, political horse trading, and policy spins to corporate donors and Beltway insiders. An example was his reversal on off shore oil drilling and dipping into the nation's petroleum reserve (he had opposed both previously). Obama did an about face on both in August, 2008 during the campaign. His explanation was simply that this was the only way to reduce gas prices and in the longer term the way to reduce foreign oil dependence. This drew accusations from rival McCain and environmentalists that he had back slid and flip flopped. The energy reversal was clearly a sop to oil interests, the rationale that he wanted to take the burden of high gas prices off consumers made his explanation for his about face plausible and palatable.

During the campaign, Obama was virtually silent on issues such as racial profiling, affirmative action, housing and job discrimination, the racial disparities in prison sentencing, and the HIV/AIDS epidemic, failing inner city schools, ending the racially-marred drug sentencing policy, and his Supreme Court appointments. He couldn't have said and done more on racial issues even if he wanted to. As the most closely watched presidential candidate in American history, he had little wiggle room to make mistakes. A lot of that was based on the fear of many of his presidency. For others, it was plainly a matter of his race. As president, he'd have even less political room to maneuver.

A president is pulled and tugged at by corporate and defense industry lobbyists, the oil and nuclear power industry, government regulators, environmental watchdog groups, conservative family values groups, moderate and conservative GOP senators and house members, foreign diplomats and leaders. They all have their priorities and agendas and all vie to get White House support for their pet legislation, or to kill or cripple legislation that threatens their interests.

The time tested rule is that liberal and moderate Democrats run to the left and move to the center when running for the White House, and stay there when they get in the White House. Obama proved no exception to that rule.

CHAPTER 2

The First 1000, Not 100 Days

emocratic Presidential contender Barack Obama made a prescient statement in October 2008. He told an interviewer on a Colorado radio station, "The first hundred days is going to be important, but it's probably going to be the first thousand days that makes the difference." Obama sounded the same sober note in campaign trail talks shortly after, repeatedly telling crowds how "hard" it would be to achieve his goals, and that it would take time. The point clearly was to damp down public expectations that he was a miracle worker. There would be no miracles in the ritual first 100 days during which the performance of new presidents is intensely scrutinized.

In tossing out the 1000 day make or break performance time frame for his presidency, candidate Obama directly parodied the line from JFK's inauguration address in 1961. Kennedy proclaimed the first 1000 days as the better time frame to measure how effective an administration is performing. Obama and JFK were wise to cite the much longer time frame. They sought to melt away the wild public expectations that they can create instant miracles.

He was well aware that the first 100 day burden would weigh heavier on him than any other president in modern times. He was young, liberal, untested, and black. There were still deep doubts, suspicions and persistent grumbles from some about his competency and political savvy. A Mt. Everest size stack of op-eds, news articles, pictorials, websites, chatrooms, national viewer polls and surveys, along with *CNN* and *MSNBC* specials which dissected, pecked apart his words and initiatives for the first 100 days, and nagged everyone else to do the same. That put even more pressure on him to show he was a tough, resolute, and effective leader.

In his quip to the Colorado radio interviewer, he knew the silliness of fixating on the drop in the bucket 100 day time span to brand a president and his presidency as a stunning success or a miserable failure. A quick look at the presidency of his two immediate predecessors was enough to prove that. Clinton bombed badly his first 100 days in office in 1992 when he tried to push Congress for a $16 billion stimulus package; he bungled the don't ask, don't tell policy regarding gays in the military, and got the first flack on his health care reform plan. Yet, the Clinton presidency is regarded as one of the most successful, popular and enduring in modern times.

His successor got off to a fast start. At the 100 day mark in April 2001, Bush's approval ratings matched Obama's. He was widely applauded for his trillion dollar tax cutting program, his "Faith-Based" and disabled Americans Initiatives, and for talking up education, health care reform and slashing the national debt. Aside from the momentary adulation he got after the 9/11 terror attack his presidency is rated as one of the worst in modern times.

* * * * *

*T*he 1000 day mark that Obama, Kennedy and other presidents have cited as the more realistic time frame for praising or damning a president is not an arbitrary number. This marks the near end of a president's first White House term. The honeymoon is long over, and the president has fought major battles over his policies, initiatives, executive orders, court appointments and programs with Congress, the courts, interest groups and the media. By that time, battles have been won, lost, or fought to a draw, and there's enough time to gauge their impact and the president's effectiveness.

The other big problem with the whimsical 100 day fixation was that it could force a president, in this case Obama, to feel that he must sprint out the gate to fulfill campaign promises, pass legislation, and burnish up his media and public credentials as a top leader. This carries risks; the risks of acting too hastily and making missteps that invite intense criticism.

He was not naïve on this score. He knew that no matter what kind of start he made there'd be criticism, lots of it. Like any savvy politician, he tried to anticipate it and then get as far ahead of the criticism as possible. This was evident in his own assessment of his first 100 days in his nationally televised press conference from the East Room of the White House April 29, 2009, "I think we're off to a good start. But it's just a start. I'm proud of what we've achieved, but I'm not content." He ticked off the problems—-terrorism, nuclear proliferation, and health care. He again returned to the theme that the better standard to determine whether he could deliver on his promises and agenda was to stretch the time in office out to a much longer time frame. That was in his words "in the second hundred days, and the third hundred days, and all the days after that."

Obama's dash to padlock the Guantanamo detention facility, announce big sweeping plans for health care, financial and banking regulation reform, his much ado about nothing handshake with Venezuelan president Hugo Chavez at the Summit of Americas conference in April 2008, his outstretch to Iran, and Cuba, and hint at dumping nuclear weapons from the world's arsenals drew heat from the right. The attack words were familiar. He was a reckless tax and spend, debt burdening, free market wrecker, and enemy conciliator. His mixed signals on prosecuting CIA torture cases and retaining virtually intact the faith based initiative, and ladling out billions to the banks drew more heat from the left that he was a backslider and Beltway politician.

The media, political pundits, supporters and attackers who clamored to grade the president on his first 100 days could not be stilled without plastering a letter grade on the major areas of policy concerns. The consensus on Obama's performance grade was remarkably similar from most experts. He got a grade from "A" to a mediocre "C" on the economy, foreign policy, Iraq, Afghanistan, health care, energy and the environment, and social issues. The broader consensus from the 100 day Obama watchers was that he didn't commit any major gaffes or blunders, and in the heated, and polarized politics in America, that in itself was a big plus for Obama. Bush also didn't commit any major gaffes or blunders during his first 100 days.

In his first presidential interview with *60 Minutes* in November, Obama told the interviewer that he took a close look at FDR's first 100 days and he was struck not by the avalanche of legislation and programs that FDR rammed through Congress his first 100 days but his willingness to do things differently. FDR is, of course, remembered, praised, and even vilified for making bold changes. In his first 100 days in office, FDR put on the table 15 major pieces of legislation. The dozens of federal programs he created are now part of American folklore. They were called "the alphabet agencies." There was the NRA, the WPA, the CCC, and the PWA; and, of course, the New Deal. The new programs that he created gave hope to millions of down and out Americans. Obama could not nor was he expected to match FDR's breath taking first 100 day performance. But then again this was not Great Depression 1930's America.

The JFK-Obama comparison was even more of a stretch. Kennedy faced no immediate foreign or domestic crisis. The better presidential comparison was with his predecessor President Bush. He is the president whose real and perceived towering White House failures helped pave the way for Obama's win. As painful as it was for some to admit it, there were some eerie similarities in the way Bush handled his first 100 days and the way Obama handled his. Bush got the same intense look in his first 100 days as Obama got in his; and for good reason. Bush's win was deeply tainted but also historic. Millions thought then and now that he won the White House through fraud, deceit, manipulation, and a huge helping hand from a politically compliant High Court. His win was historic and tinged with racial and ideological fears. Though the Bush legacy is truly dreadful, it wasn't that way at the start. He got the same first 100 days pass from voters that Obama and every other president has gotten. His April 2001 poll numbers topped sixty percent. This matched Obama's April 2009 numbers. A *Washington Post/ABC* Poll even gave Bush high marks on his handling of the economy. Bush did what every other new president did during his first hundred days. He used the early public goodwill to make politically favorable appointments, ink executive orders and shove through Congress programs that likely would draw fire later on, clamp a vise like grip on executive power, and cast an eye on cementing his historic legacy.

Bush introduced a $1.6 trillion tax cutting program to Congress, launched a "Faith-Based" Initiative to help local charitable groups, and "New Freedom" Initiative to help disabled Americans. In his first address to Congress, he cast himself as the education president, talked about health care reform, and made a vague promise to tackle paying off the national debt. Obama followed pretty much the same script. Bush worked hard to dispel the notion that he was a foreign policy neophyte, topped by his widely ridiculed stumble in not knowing the name of Pakistan's president. He quickly met or talked with dozens of foreign leaders and diplomats. They included all of Latin America's leaders. The one exception was Fidel Castro. Obama also took big campaign hits for being a foreign policy novice and moved just as quickly to meet and talk with foreign leaders. The same exception was Cuban leaders Fidel Castro and brother Raul. Bush took a stab at bipartisanship when he let stand a Clinton administration rule that would expand acres of wetlands across the United States, and ended a long running trade dispute over bananas with the European Union. He hinted that he would take seriously the Kyoto accords on climate warming, reduce the use of coal burning plants, and tighten regulation on toxic chemicals in water supplies. He reneged on every one of them. He still paid lip service to them. Obama talked about making these issues and problems priority items of his administration too.

* * * * *

*A*quick casualty was one of Bush's more controversial executive orders. That was the reinstatement of the Mexico City policy denying US aid to countries that advocate abortion as a method of family planning. Anti-abortion advocates hailed Bush for imposing the ban. Abortion advocates hailed Obama for overturning it.

Bush's most controversial cabinet appointment was the religious fundamentalist leaning John Ashcroft as Attorney General. Obama picked Eric Holder as Attorney General. This also stirred some controversy over partisanship and ideology. Holder was hammered by some GOP hardliners for being a point man for the wheels and deals that went in to getting Clinton pardons of convicted financier and key Democratic Party bankroller Marc Rich during Holder's stint as Deputy Attorney General.

Bush staunchly backed a national missile defense system in Europe. Obama to an extent backed it too. In a speech in the Czech Republic in April, 2009, he called a missile defense system in that country and Poland the most cost-effective and proven defense system. He tied the decision to go ahead with it directly to Iran's nuclear threat and international security concerns. Critics hotly disputed the need for the system when Bush backed it. They disputed the need for it when Obama called for it. He later scrapped it.

Near the close of his first 100 days Bush told an audience at the annual Radio and Television Correspondents Association dinner that the world was a dangerous place; it was us versus them. Then he paused and admitted that he wasn't really sure who the "them" was. Bush was wildly cheered at the dinner. America's love fest with him was still in full bloom. It didn't last. FDR, JFK and every other president's immediate post election popularity high didn't last either.

Obama hedged his bets that the impatience of millions of Americans who believed his promise of change would see immediate results wouldn't just a quickly sour on him. He told a Georgetown University audience in April 2009, "I know how difficult it is for members of Congress in both parties to grapple with some of the big decisions we face right now. It's more than most Congresses and most presidents have to deal with in a lifetime. But we have been called to govern in extraordinary times."

His plea for patience and time along with his admonition for the same in the Colorado interview near the close of the campaign was simply his way of saying that no president's on the job performance can be fairly measured against his campaign promises in a few months time. Politics and events simply didn't work that neatly in a 100 days, or maybe even in a 1000 days. However, at least by the end of 1000 days Americans would certainly know a lot more about the man they put in the White House than in the ceremonial but meaningless 100 days.

CHAPTER 3

Waging Bush's Terror War

Former Vice President Dick Cheney minced no words in defending his boss, former president Bush's war on terror policy, "If it hadn't been for what we did - with respect to the terrorist surveillance program, or enhanced interrogation techniques for high-value detainees, the Patriot Act, and so forth - then we would have been attacked again. Those policies we put in place, in my opinion, were absolutely crucial to getting us through the last seven-plus years without a major-casualty attack on the US." Cheney spat out virtually the same uncompromising no-apology for Bush's war in talks, interviews, and articles in the first months after Obama took office.

His hard nosed defense was less to defend what Bush and he did in the anti-terror war then a snipe at Obama. Cheney was horrified at the thought that Obama would actually deliver on his campaign promises to wage the war on terror totally different. The implication was that there would be no more illegal wiretaps, prison dungeons, indefinite sentences, military summary military trials, and most importantly the use of torture. Obama vowed publicly to close the terrorist holding pen at Guantanamo which had become a universal symbol of the worst US abuses in the anti-terror war. This appeared to indicate that Obama would make good on his promise to do things radically different than Bush in the waging the anti-terrorism war.

Obama left little doubt about that when he lashed back at Cheney in a *CBS Sixty Minutes* interview in March 2009, "How many terrorists have actually been brought to justice under the philosophy that is being promoted by Vice president Cheney?" The implication was that Bush made a mockery of international law and rule through the deliberate use of torture and endless detention of terror suspects with no charges being brought or trials held. The painful reality was that despite Obama's pledge to scrap Bush's terror policy there were still far too many points where his policy resembled Bush's policy. In the waning days of his last term Bush dumped some of the worst of the legally and morally obscene interrogation tactics. He partially emptied the bulging cells of terror suspects at Guantanamo. He even tried to make overtures of conciliation to the European allies who vehemently opposed US torture tactics. The courts ruled that the Bush administration grossly violated constitutional and legal precepts by scooping up and holding terror suspects on flimsy evidence with no charges or trials.

The Bush shifts and changes dovetailed with Obama's position on getting rid of the most blatant abuses. But he didn't go much further than that. During the presidential campaign he strongly hinted that he'd eliminate most if not all of Bush's executive orders that infringed on civil liberties rights and protections in the war on terror and the Iraq war. There were 31 in all.

The best known and most controversial was the executive order that granted wide latitude in loosely defining what and who is a "terrorist combatant," where and how long that individual could be held (indefinitely) and how they should be legally disposed of (none of the standard constitutional protections).

Bush didn't stop there. He issued Executive Order 13440 in July 2007. The order was deliberately vague and did not spell out what interrogation practices were permissible. The order gave the green light to interrogators to dodge the safeguards spelled out in the Geneva Convention against illegal and inhumane treatment of prisoners. The military took the cue and didn't miss a beat in their prisoner interrogations. That was only the most naked example of using an executive order to subvert the law. More than two dozen other executive orders that Bush signed into law and that quickly became operational between 2005 and early 2008 slipped far under the public radar scope and got little if any public attention but were just as abusive.

* * * * *

Bush signed another executive order the same week he signed the executive order that subverted the Supreme Court's ruling in July, 2007 against him on prisoner interrogation practices. That order blocked the sale and transfer of property of any individual deemed a threat to the stabilization efforts in Iraq. In other words, anyone who spoke out against the Iraq War could in theory be branded a terrorist and have their property seized. This legally dubious executive order received passing press mention and little scrutiny from lawmakers. As far as is known the executive order is still on the books.

It was still subject to individual interpretation of who is a terrorist (suspect) and who makes that determination. The courts didn't make that determination. The core of the Bush terrorism war firmly embedded in the executive orders that permit suspects to be held without trial, gives the military the right to determine what interrogation tactics can be used and when, and reinforces the paranoid secrecy that encases the military's dealing with terror suspects. The executive orders were clearly designed to make it near impossible for suspects to get their full complement of legal rights and protections. Under Bush policy, even targeted killings of terrorists wherever they were or deemed to be, was sanctioned.

Obama did not change that policy. Nor did he fully reverse Bush's patently illegal domestic surveillance policies. CIA director designate Leon Panetta gave a big tip that much of Bush's war on terror policies would remain untouched during his Senate confirmation hearings in February 2007. He admitted that if the approved techniques were "not sufficient" to get a terrorism suspect to supply information about a presumed terror attack he would seek "additional authority." This was a polite euphemism for applying torture.

Bush made a deliberate legal morass of the terrorism war, and his executive orders horribly show that. Cheney's media crusade to rap Obama and absolve himself and his boss from legal and moral culpability for their abuses didn't change that. Yet, some of Cheney's charges about Obama's embrace of Bush policy on the terror war were not that far off the mark.

* * * * *

*H*is decision in May 2009 not to release the appalling photos of the torture of Iraqi prisoners didn't do much to convince people that he had done a sharp about face from Bush in the terror war. The telling thing about Obama's response to Army General Ray Odierno's impassioned plea to him not to release the photos was not that he gave in to the general. It was what he said to the general when he made the decision. The general asked, "It must have been a hard decision," Obama's answer, "No, it wasn't at all."

This was not hyperbole to appease a fawning, jittery, hard nosed general. Nor was it a chronic case of backsliding, flip-flopping, or betrayal of principle. Obama recognized that many widely suspected that he'd be spineless on national security and military toughness. He was determined to prove the skeptics wrong. National security and military toughness aren't simply politically volatile issues. They've been the political Achilles Heel of Democrats.

Democratic presidents and presidential candidates starting with Clinton have done everything they could to wrap a protective guard around that heel. To do that they had to snatch a page from the GOP playbook that requires them to talk tough on national security and military preparedness. In countless speeches and private talks during the 2000 presidential campaign, Clinton sternly warned the Democrats that if they wanted to grab the White House they must seize the national security and defense issues from the Republicans. That meant doing and saying nothing that stirs public sensibilities and fears on the war on terrorism and about Democratic military softness. At times, it meant trying to out Bush Bush on the GOP's stock issue of the war on terrorism and national security.

Democratic presidential contenders Al Gore and John Kerry took Clinton's advice to heart with disastrous results. They both tried to strike the tough guy pose. Kerry even said at one point that he'd launch preemptive strikes against terrorists wherever they were and that he would launch search and destroy missions to ferret out Osama Bin Laden and Al-Qaeda leaders. Their talk fooled absolutely no one. Endless polls showed that the voters repeatedly gave Bush huge percentage margins over Kerry when asked who they thought would do a better job in the anti-terror war.

Kerry didn't understand the futility of his tough guy stance. He kept slamming Bush as being, weak and ineffective in fighting terrorism. He touted his military credentials as a Vietnam combat vet to supposedly prove that he would and could be every bit if not more the hardliner on terrorism than Bush, to no vote getting avail.

* * * * *

During the campaign, with only slight stylistic tweaks, Obama pretty much followed the same playbook as Kerry. He really had no choice. He was viciously baited on the sound of his name, slandered and lied about as a Muslim, and pounded for allegedly not wearing an American flag in his lapel and not hoisting his hand to his heart when the national anthem was played. In the minds of many suspicious Americans, that typed him as inherently questionable on being a stalwart tough guy on terrorism and national defense, and worse unpatriotic. These were all attack points during the campaign for various McCain, Sarah Palin, Republican National Committee, and packs of conservative bloggers.

McCain waved his credentials as Bush did as the man who Americans wanted in the driver's seat to safeguard national security. The not so subtle message was that Obama wasn't that man. The polls backed up McCain on that claim. Most found that nearly half of Americans said he was not hard-nosed enough on national security and McCain was. That of course, raised hackles among Team Obama and they took great pains to assert their military preparedness credentials. Once in office, liberals grumbled that Obama backpedaled on his promises to totally dismantle the most odious of Bush's torture policies and that included hauling Bush officials accused of condoning torture and illegal wiretapping into a court docket.

The failure to fully reverse Bush torture policies had nothing to do with Obama's merely putting pragmatism over principle, especially since a federal judge had already ordered the photos released. The photos were even then being widely circulated on the web. More importantly, America's enemies are certainly well aware of and have experienced first hand the full brunt of CIA and military dirty tactics.

His refusal to release the photos was another instance of a moderate Democratic president under the intense glare of the military and GOP looking glass doing the politically expedient and necessary thing and that's to kiss the ring of national security and military resolve. The message that the administration would tread carefully and at times tough on the politically volatile issue of national security was conveyed speedily to Attorney General Eric Holder. That was still the most troubling and contentious issue of whether Obama should green light the prosecution of Bush officials for illegal activities.

* * * * *

*T*hings didn't seem very promising on that score when Holder told Utah Senator Orrin Hatch during his confirmation hearing in January 2009 that he would not prosecute any Bush officials for authorizing dubious wiretapping. Holder had little choice in the matter. The prosecutions would bog down the Obama administration in an all consuming ultimately no win factional fight with Congressional Republicans, the courts—especially the Supreme Court which upheld Bush provisions authorizing torture, and lots of holdover Bush Justice Department and civil rights division-appointed attorneys. There were few squeals from Congressional leaders at Bush's borderline legal and constitutionally dubious executive orders that permitted the long checklist of civil liberties abuses, warrantless wiretaps of U.S. citizens, being one of the more glaring. Holder did not make administration policy. He just articulated it.

In a terse statement three months later, Obama ended all speculation and the hopes of civil libertarian and civil rights groups that he might haul one or more Bush officials into court for lawbreaking, "This is a time for reflection, not retribution. I respect the strong views and emotions that these issues evoke. We have been through a dark and painful chapter in our history. But at a time of great challenges and disturbing disunity, nothing will be gained by spending our time and energy laying blame for the past." That didn't end the clamor for prosecutions. Obama and Holder continued to get pilloried for letting Bush officials skip away scot free for their alleged crimes. Obama slightly buckled and made one small concession

In August 2009, Holder announced that he had ordered "a preliminary review into whether federal laws were violated in connection with the interrogation of specific detainees at overseas locations." Holder was careful to note this was only a fact finding review not a full blown investigation with no timetable on its completion, and no plan to prosecute anyone found to, in his words, who failed to "act in good faith and *within the scope of legal guidance."* Seven former CIA directors promptly screamed foul. They sternly warned that any full blown investigation would have a chilling effect on future CIA operations. This almost certainly meant that Holder would limit the scope of the investigation to only what the bottom rung small fry CIA operatives did. This hardly rose to the standard of sweeping investigations, let alone prosecutions of Bush officials. There were reports that some White House aides privately expressed discomfort with even this tepid move by Holder.

That was only part of the reason why Holder was seemingly willing to let bygones be bygones when it came to prosecuting Bush's crew members for their blatant civil liberties abuses. The other part was that it would pry open again the Democrats dirty but hardly unknown secret. When word leaked out about the scope and complexity of the warrantless wiretap program before the 2006 midterm elections Congressional Democrats not only did nothing about it, they aided and abetted the Bush administration in approving the illegal spying.

The Democratic-controlled Congress passed the "Protect America Act." This put the Congressional stamp of approval on what Bush did and actually expanded his powers to snoop. The targets weren't just foreign terror suspects and known operatives but American citizens. Democrats knew this and approved it by inserting in the law open-ended wording that permitted legalized spying on anyone outside the U.S. who intelligence agencies "reasonably believed" to possess foreign intelligence information.

The law deliberately made no distinction about exactly who the target could be. Another clause granted immunity from lawsuits to the communications service providers that made Bush snooping possible. With no fear or threat of legal action against the companies, the wraps were legally off on who could be snooped on. As an added sweetener, the law also gave Bush emergency power to tap for up to a week anyone deemed a terror threat; all without a warrant. This didn't end matters.

* * * * *

In January 2008 then Democratic presidential contenders Obama and Hillary Clinton flatly said that they were so troubled by the Foreign Services Intelligence Act which essentially slapped a cloak of immunity over the telecommunications companies that were the key to running the warrantless tapping. They said the Act was far too weak in providing protections against the rampant abuses in domestic intelligence gathering operations. The issue again was the virtual nonexistent controls on warrantless wiretapping and the provision that granted immunity to telecommunications companies who engaged in the reckless and borderline lawless surveillance of any and everyone tagged as a potential terrorist threat.

Clinton and Obama vowed that they would not support the bill with the dangerous lack of civil liberties safeguards. Both initially voted no on cloture. Clinton kept her word and voted no in the vote on the final passage of the bill. Most of the top Democrats with few exceptions caved and backed it. Obama was one of them. He softened the reversal of his prior opposition to FISA with the vague hint that he might make some changes at another point in time, ""Given the legitimate threats we face, providing effective intelligence collection tools with appropriate safeguards is too important to delay. So I support the compromise, but do so with a firm pledge that as president, I will carefully monitor the program."

Holder told Hatch in his confirmation hearing that he didn't want to criminalize policy differences that may exist between the Bush administration and the Obama administration. He was right especially when as the record clearly showed that more than a few top Democrats were deeply complicit making sure that those differences were not differences at all. That included to the bitter disappointment of many civil liberties groups, President Obama.

CHAPTER 4

It Was Still the Economy, Stupid

*V*ice President Joe Biden said with a confident smile and nod on September 3, 2009 that the nearly $800 billion that Obama pumped into a stimulus program was not only working, but working better and faster than planned. Biden didn't stop with a hearty back pat of the administration. He boasted that the stimulus was the single biggest reason the US averted a full blown 1930's style Great Depression. This was much more than over-inflated political hyperbole. He had to say something and say something fast about the alleged miracle economic curative power of the stimulus. A *Washington Post* poll taken the same week found that a big majority of Americans disputed Biden's assessment and said that the stimulus hadn't done anything to jumpstart the economy.

A *Gallup Poll* also released at the same time that Biden cheered the stimulus was awash in public gloom. A majority said Obama had spent too much of taxpayer money and gotten too little in return by way of a decisive economic rebound. Even more ominous, nearly one in four believed the stimulus made the economy worse.

The disconnect between Biden's rosy view of the stimulus and much of the public's malignant view of it was just as evident in the duels between economists over the stimulus's value. Some argued it helped to boost consumer confidence, sparked a rise in stock prices and stirred a slight jump in housing sales. Others insisted it was much too soon to say the economy had truly bottomed out and it was on the rise. Democrats were mostly silent but still hopeful that the stimulus had done what Obama said it would do.

Republicans continued to sound the warning that the stimulus was too big, wasteful and ineffectual. They claimed that it pushed the deficit through the ceiling and made government even more intrusive than ever.

The stimulus was the trigger for the continuing debate over where the economy should go. It masked a deeper unease and public worry that too much money was going to too many places with little accountability, and transparency. And worse, the stimulus was benefiting many of the people who had created the economic mess. In a weekly radio and Internet address in July 2009, Obama vented some of his frustration and irritation over the carping of the critics, "When we passed this Recovery Act, there were those who felt that doing nothing was somehow an answer," he said. "Today, some of those same critics are already judging the effort a failure although they have yet to offer a plausible alternative."

From the start, he banked heavily on his top economic advisor pick, Lawrence Summers to mend fences, soothe ruffle feathers, and assuage the critics of the stimulus plan. Summers was in a unique position to do that. He was the consummate Wall Street insider. His resume read like a mini telephone book on the list of posts he'd held in and out of every financial and government monetary agency imaginable. Any other time, he would and probably should have been hailed as the apt pick for Obama to turn to for help in sorting out some of the economic chaos. Summers' role, though, in helping create some of the economic problems raised a red flag.

Simply revisiting the part he played in creating some of the havoc didn't answer the even more compelling question and that's: Did Summers and indeed other Team Obama's economic advisors, most of them old Bill Clinton administration officials, still see the prescription for financial health that they peddled to Clinton in the 1990s as the same prescription for ultimately solving the nation's economic woes a decade later?

By the time Summers and other key Obama economic advisors took the reins in 2009, it was well documented that Bush and the Republicans had eagerly cut sweetheart deals with financial industry lobbyists to gut lending and stock trading regulations, winked and nodded at the banks and brokerage houses as they engaged in an orgy of dubious stock swapping, buys, and trading, conned millions of homeowners into taking out catastrophic sub prime loans and watered down the oversight powers of government regulatory agencies.

Summers and Robert Rubin, the other key advisor, both served as Clinton's Treasury secretaries. They lobbied Clinton and Congress hard in the late 1990s to dump most of the provisions of the decades old Glass-Steagall Act. The Act was the 1930s Great Depression era measure that kept federally insured banks out of the go-go world of stock trading and exotic lending and financial speculation. It also set rigid standards for mortgage lending and strict oversight over banking practices.

The rationale for scrapping the Act was that U.S. banks and brokerage houses needed to have the restrictions snatched off to stay competitive with Asian and European bankers and financial traders. President Clinton bought the line. The revision bill passed with bipartisan support in 1999 and Clinton quickly signed it. In an interview in October 2008, Clinton still was unapologetic about signing the legislation. He did not see that it caused any financial dislocation and defended it vigorously against the critics, including then candidate Obama, "On the Glass-Steagall thing, if you could demonstrate to me that it was a mistake, I'd be glad to look at the evidence.

"But I can't blame [the Republicans]. This wasn't something they forced me into. I really believed that given the level of oversight of banks and their ability to have more patient capital, if you made it possible for [commercial banks] to go into the investment banking business as Continental European investment banks could always do, that it might give us a more stable source of long-term investment."

* * * * *

That was only part of the financial deal cutting between the banks and Clinton and Congress. A year later Summers in tandem with then Texas GOP senator and Chair of the Senate Banking Committee Phil Gramm rammed through another "financial modernization" measure. This one took the wraps off government regulations that checked banks, insurance companies and brokerage houses from pumping billions into financial swaps (speculation) on commodities such as oil and food staples. The rationale was the same as that given for getting rid of Glass-Steagall and that it was passed to keep the financial institutions as full profit centers with minimal to no government oversight accountability or investor, depositor and shareholder accountability.

The predictable quickly happened with the regulatory gloves off commercial banks, brokerage firms, hedge funds, institutional investors, pension funds and insurance companies did whatever they wanted when it came to investing in each other's businesses and marching in lock step with each other's financial operations. Yet, barely a week after Obama was elected president; a buoyant Summers called the revamp of the financial industry as "the legislative foundation of the financial system of the 21st century."

The question that hung precariously in the air was did Summers think that the implosion of Wall Street which directly resulted from the terrible policies that he and other Clinton financial experts orchestrated a decade ago and that led to so much waste, misery and bickering was still a fit model for righting the economic ship? Democratic House Speaker Nancy Pelosi evidently thought so. She raised a red flag when she couldn't say enough good things about Summers and other former Clinton officials and the cast of Wall Street connected advisors that Team Obama had called back into service to right the economic ship.

Obama continued to hear the complaints and continued to hit back. On September 14, 2009, the first anniversary of the collapse of the ancient Wall Street brokerage firm Lehman Bros, he spoke at Fed-

eral Hall in the heart of Wall Street. He talked tough about including new consumer protection rules that included closing regulator
loopholes, tight policing and oversight of financial transactions, and
limiting executive pay.

The tough talk came amidst reports that the big five banks
Goldman Sachs, JP Morgan Chase, Wells Fargo, Citigroup and Bank
of America in the second quarter of 2008 posted bigger, fatter, and
to the rage of much of the public, more inflated profits than the year
before the financial collapse and the federal bailout. Even as he spoke
and the G20 nations were scheduled to meet the following week in
Pittsburgh, there were still loud warnings that Obama's tough talk
about new controls over Wall Street had fallen on deaf Wall Street
ears.

Joseph Stiglitz, former chief economist of the World Bank, flatly
said the banking problems were bigger and more serious than before
the Wall Street meltdown, and that beyond talk about tougher regulatory oversight neither Obama or Congress had done little to put
teeth into monitoring Wall Street's still risky wheel and deal invest-
ments and speculation.

Another red flag on the economy was the action of Senate Democrats. They helped to kill a bill in 2005 that would have re-imposed
some constraints on the financial industry. The reason was the same
as before; any limitation would stifle its ability to compete. However,
this time, public anger over Wall Street greed and malfeasance had
drastically changed the Senate's tune at least outwardly about regu-
lating the financial industry. The proof of how tough Congress was
really going to be on the industry was not in talk, but action.

At a press conference in January 2009, Obama unveiled his economic team. He assured that his team offered "sound judgment and fresh thinking" to deal with the dire economic peril. Time would tell just how sound the judgment was in formulating measures to combat the financial meltdown.

* * * * *

*T*he concern over their performance was not due soley to public jitters over the economy in Obama's first year. There were the terrible memories of how badly Bush mangled the economy, and the crucial importance of the economy to the daily lives of American's and the political lives of politicians and presidents.

From the first day of the presidential campaign the enshrined article of political faith was that voters were so furious at Bush for causing massive plant closings, farm failures, corporate bungling, fraud and corruption, the housing collapse, soaring gas prices, and the wholesale flight and disappearance of jobs, that all a Democratic presidential contender had to do to win election was pass the breath test on Election Day. It was never that simple. It was not always the economy that made or broke presidents. In a look at how six of eight presidents fared since 1948 when the economy hit the skids or appeared to skid, the scorecard for presidents winning and losing because of economic woe is a draw. Three were beaten and three beat back their challengers. It came down to whether voters really perceived that their economic plight, or degree of pain, would show no sign of a cure if they kept the incumbent in office.

Republican and Democratic presidents won and lost elections even when there was widespread public unease over the economy and many voters believed things wouldn't get any better. The presidents who won had to do one important thing in the face of rising unemployment, recession, inflation, and public fears. They had to assure a majority of voters that things would and could get better with them if they stayed in the White House and their opponent couldn't do any better than they had done in the White House.

The combination of real and perceived voter economic woe helped sink Presidents Gerald Ford and Bush Sr. It helped and hurt Carter. It helped when the economy went bad for Ford in 1976 allowing Carter to win a narrow victory over Ford. The trick was that voters had to perceive things would get worse in which case the challenger to a sitting president had to reinforce public dread that things would indeed get worse.

Four years later, when the economy went bad for Carter, Reagan won in a near landslide. The exact reverse was true for Reagan and Bill Clinton. Reagan's supply side economics and big tax cuts were credited with igniting a mid-1980s economic boom. Clinton's tax hike, deficit reduction program, and investment stimulus program, was credited with turning a record deficit into a record surplus and adding millions of new jobs to the rolls.

As Reagan's vice president, Bush Sr. benefited from his economic policies. In 1988, he won the election. Four years later, when things turned bad he lost. It's not just a bad economy, though, that determines the fate of incumbet presidents it's the actual point in time that the economy turns bad during the president's term. It's also whether the public perceives that things will get better or worse for them if his administration stays in power. The downturn for Bush Sr. came during the last two years of his term. Voters are much more likely to blame and punish a president if they go to the polls with economic doubts fresh in their minds.

Bush Sr.'s history did not repeat itself with W. Bush in the 2004 election. Even though unemployment was high, and economic growth, as Democrats gleefully noted, was slower than during Clinton's second term, the Clinton bar was impossibly high to match anyway. By all economic standards, his economic track record was the best of any of the last five presidents. Even by Clinton's high standard of success , and despite the industrial erosion in some sections of the country, during the last two years of and economic growth still slightly improved.

This was the powerful spur that Bush used to spin news, even bad economic news, as a gain. He solemnly pledged there would be more economic goodies for voters if he was reelected. If the economic negatives had hit harder in his last two years, as it did with his father, it would have been Democratic presidential John Kerry's ticket to the White House.

In the twilight hours of the Bush presidency things went from bad to worse. The lesson wasn't lost on Obama. It was the "it's the economy stupid" political axiom all over again. This was the big reason that Obama stacked his economic team with Clinton seasoned and Wall Street connected insiders. They could calm the nerves of Wall Street bankers, investment houses, and corporate CEOs who wanted assurances that Obama would not impose draconian, heavy handed regulations, and do little to end the much reviled bonuses and perks they laddled out to their CEOs. They especially wanted assurance that he would not impose hefty tax hikes on the wealthy and corporations, and implement massive FDR style government spending on job and public works programs. And finally, they wanted reassurance that he would continue to pump billions into the coffers of the top banks with few regulatory strings attached.

The usual critics, progressives, labor radicals, populist Democrats, and doctrinaire free market conservatives continued to lambaste this as not a prescription for economic recovery but a giveaway to the banks and corporations. If it worked to the extent that the economy did not sink too far, or better still stabilized, then Obama would get the credit. It would prove the point again that presidents who don't make too big a mess of the economy are immently reelectable. However, with the economy still on shaky ground through much of 2009 and with some predictions that the ground would remain unstable in 2010, it was far too early to make predictions about the political fate of the White House. Obama clearly had tied a big part of his political future to the turnaround of the economy and to his team's effort to turn it around. It was still the economy, stupid.

CHAPTER 5

A Red President

*I*n a feature *Esquire* interview in July 2009 former Florida Governor Jeb Bush was asked, "Is Obama a socialist?" Bush's short answer, "I don't know." His answer was as duplicitous as it was cryptic. Bush, GOP operatives, and legions of conservative bloggers, and talk radio jocks worked tirelessly through the presidential campaign to tar Obama as a stealth red president out to socialize medicine, snatch wealth from the rich and middle class, impose a Joe Stalin style big and repressive government on America, and reorder capitalism.

Midway through the presidential campaign in October 2008 Republican rival McCain egged on by *the Fox News Network*'s hourly assault on Obama grabbed at a horribly outdated interview in 2001 in which then Illinois Senator Obama told a Chicago radio station that he favored "redistributive change." He mildly rebuked the Supreme Court for not doing more to make that happen. McCain and Fox screamed that this was socialism. Obama's point was that breaking down the barriers of Jim Crow segregation was a pyrhic victory without decent jobs and income for poor blacks and Latinos. Civil rights leaders for years said pretty much the same thing; that the goal of the civil rights movement revolution was incomplete without an economic boost to the poor. McCain's overt red tar of Obama got almost no traction.

However, McCain, undaunted by the media and public's relative cool shoulder to his innuendo that Obama advocated socialist wealth redistribution, had another red ploy. That was Obama's fleeting and peripheral one time association with former Weather Underground terrorist William Ayers, now turned into a respected University professor. In an April 2008 *ABC-TV* interview, McCain didn't hestiate when asked about Ayers and the infererence that Obama's patriotism was suspect, "I'm sure he's patriotic. But his relationship with Mr. Ayers is open to question." By the attack standards of the far right, it was bland and tepid.

McCain's VP running mate, Sarah Palin, had no such restraint. In an October 2008 *CNN* interview she cited the instant conservative expert, Joe the Plumber, to smear Obama as a socialist, *"I'm not going to call him a socialist but as Joe the plumber has suggested, in fact, he came right out and said it, it sounds like socialism to him* and he speaks for so many Americans who are quite concerned now after hearing finally what Barack Obama's true intentions are with his tax and economic plan."

Palin had picked up on the Ohio plumber's apoplectic reaction to Obama's off the cuff, and terribly out of context quip to his question in a campaign stop in Ohio in October 2008 about the economy and taxes that he stood for as redistributing the wealth. McCain quickly jumped back to the attack in a radio address and acted as Perry Mason getting a suspect to confess on the witness stand. This was tantamount to smoking gun proof for him that Obama was a socialist. It was no such thing. The 11th hour attack sounded more and more like the desperate raving of a beaten and spent candidate who was going nowhere in the polls and at the ballot box.

This didn't stop the swelling pack of bloggers, web pundits, and conservative talk jocks from taking up the McCain and Palin chant that Obama was a closet red. They took off on the alleged Obama-Ayers tie and launched a shrill campaign of Kremlin comparison taunts and baiting of Obama. Obama's big spending plan to ratchet up the economy, pay for jobs, expanded education and health care, and to hit the rich harder to pay for these sent them into hysteria. By late September 2008 with the Wall Street meltdown, a looming full blown economic collapse, and the public blaming much of this on Bush and the GOP, it was clear that the red smear of Obama was no more than a minor annoyance. But the seed had been planted.

The smear was a cunning, calculated and a formula political gambit that could be used repeatedly to keep the Obama administration off balance. In the months after his inauguration in January, 2009, the right side bloggers, chatters, and talk radio gabbers piled tons of anti Obama slurs and slams on websites, blogs and articles.

* * * * *

Meanwhile GOP leaders continued to plant carefully calibrated digs that Obama posed a clear and present danger to the free market and private enterprise, "This is a massive movement of the government to the left," railed New Hampshire Senator Judd Gregg, a Senate budget expert who briefly flirted with joining Obama's cabinet.

There was some evidence that the red attacks actually produced some results. In an August 2009 *US News and World Report* poll nearly 90 percent of the respondents said that Obama's policies were socialist. There were more than 2 million references (and climbing during the month), quotes, quips, comments, and notations on Obama as a socialist on Google in that month. The sheer mass of anti Obama slanders from the right, the fringe and the GOP operatives forced much of the mainstream media and respected commentators, analysts and bloggers who should've known better to spend time and space arguing the cons of the claim and refuting it. This gave back door credence to the charge.

The irony was that then candidate Obama also gave backdoor validity to the socialist attacks during a rally in Raleigh, North Carolina in October 2009. He mocked the charge in a blast at McCain after he strongly hinted there was a red taint to his agenda. He laughed it off saying "what's next calling me a communist." Unfortunately, there were more than a few who were eager to say just that about him.

Even if Obama ignored the charges, and the GOP had played it on the up and up and stuck to the standard attack on Democrats as pro tax and spend, big government, and dovish on defense, Obama still would have been branded a socialist by many ultra conservatives. It's a juicy term that touches a raw nerve with most Americans who are in a fog on what socialism is and how it works as a system. To many Americans a socialist is someone who is pro union, for increased government spending on health and education programs, and a strong backer of civil liberities and civil rights protections. This always drew fire from the right. During the 1960's Dr. Martin Luther King, Jr. was routinely smeared as a communist and socialist.

The mildest criticism of big business and the wealthy by a candidate, an elected official and even a president draws instant cries of socialism from opponents. The American economic sacred cow is that *laissez faire* wealth is tantamount to a divine right of kings and any attempt to touch it is economic heresy. Politicians know that it is a kiss of death to be seen as an advocate for tax and income fairness. That invites being plastered with the socialist tag.

GOP presidents and presidential candidates ritually play the tax and spend card to brand their Democratic rivals as dangers to middle-class wage earners. This stokes fear that underneath the Democrat's tax and spend policies that supposedly target the rich the undeserving poor will be the sole beneficiaries. The scare of wealth redistribution has worked in the past precisely because wealth and income iniquities are so great in America. The notion that there's nothing wrong with the iniquities is deeply entrenched in tax policy, philosophy and politics. Obama quickly found out just how deep when he took the predictable heat from conservatives and to his surprise from some liberals when he called for a marginal tax increase on high income earners to finance part of the estimated $1 trillion cost for his health care reform plan. A chagrined Obama couched the plea for the tax increase in the narrowest frame. He insisted that it was needed solely to damp down medical cost inflation. This didn't quiet the complaints that tax hikes were a ploy by liberals and radicals to soak the rich.

Any talk of putting more wealth into the hands of the nonwealthy in the way of tax cuts, a Social Security tax increase on upper income wage earners, capital gains increases, and closing tax shelter loopholes is plainly regarded as wealth redistribution downward. During the presidential campaign, McCain grabbed at the formula that GOP contenders traditionally use and hit Obama with it.

Democrats and Independent politicians from FDR to Huey Long to Ralph Nader have railed against the top heavy wealth of the relative handful. FDR excepted, they have been routinely branded as crackpots or socialists, and then quickly politically marginalized. In his wink and nod hint that there was a red taint to Obama, McCain simply snatched at the formula that GOP contenders have typically used.

It works to the extent that it has because millions of middle and working class wage earners dream that they will be rich someday and are horrified that they can have their imagined wealth downsized by a tax and spend Democrat or worse a Democrat who's branded as socialist leaning.

During the campaign Obama cringed in horror at the absurd notion that he is a wait-in-the wings Marxist. But tossing the damaging political label at him was more than just a last desperate gasp effort by the GOP to get an edge on him. It tapped into the broad belief and even fear that Obama can and will actually stiff the rich and by extension those who fantasize about being rich. The question, "Is Obama a Socialist" may have seemed silly. Yet, to even ask it created just enough doubt. That suited the GOP which wasted no time in subtly dropping even stronger hints about Obama's supposed radical leanings.

* * * * *

*I*n quick succession in February 2009, South Carolina Senator Jim DeMint, one time Republican presidential candidate Mike Huckabee, and the more extreme House Republicans, Michelle Bachman and Zach Wamp lambasted President Obama as the second coming of V.I. Lenin for floating a mild plan to marginally increase taxes on the highest income earners to help pay for his health reform plan.

The irony was that a *Fox News Network* poll the next month found that by a big margin Americans said that making the rich pay a bigger share of their income in taxes wasn't a bad idea. They agreed that the tax system is way out of whack and that those from the Wall Street fast buck artists to tax dodging corporate executives wallow in obscene wealth while the poor get poorer and the middle-class get soaked. Even a majority of Republicans agree that the rich can and should pay more. Still, the red baiting continued to have some resonance in the media. The *Los Angeles Times, New York Times, Washington Post*, and the *Chicago Tribune* periodically touched on the issue in articles on various controversies that swirled around Obama's economic and health care reform policies.

DeMint, Huckabee, and the fringe Republicans were well aware that the socialism was a red herring that could instantly raise emotional hackles and suspicions of big segments on Americans. This could muddy public policy debates. This was likely to be the case on the inherently divisive and contentious issues of taxes, spending, and the role and size of government.

Obama ridiculed all such talk that his economic program was out of the pale and mocked GOP talk show jock Rush Limbaugh who through 2009 turned his daily talk show into a virtual on-air counterinsurgent organizing vehicle to whip up sentiment against the supposed socialist leaning tax and spend Obama.

Obama, however, did not fall completely into the trap again and dignify the socialist smear as he did at his campaign rally in Raleigh, North Carolina in October 2008. He knew that to answer the charge again was tantamount to trying to answer the ancient lose-lose question when did you stop beating your wife? No matter how much he mocked, ridiculed, and laughed away the charge, it would not change the mind of even one anti-Obama true believer that he was a wealth distributing, big government radical. It certainly wouldn't do anything to dissuade the GOP operatives from continuing to slap the label on him.

In a July 2009 talk at the Washington D.C. National Press Club, Republican National Committee Chair Michael Steele went on the Obama as socialist attack again. When asked if Obama's health care plan represented socialism, Steele responded: "Yes, next question."

Steele brusquely shifted gears in the questioning. His equally brusque answer left no doubt that the "Is Obama a Socialist" question (and answer) was deeply embedded in the GOP's arsenal of below the belt weapons to snipe, hector, and stir public doubts about Obama on his economic initiatives and health care reform. This even troubled some conservatives. In an exclusive *CNN* interview in September 2009, former First Lady Laura Bush bristled at calling Obama a socialist. She called it "unfair."

It was. But the socialist tag, like the other political hit terms such as , soft on crime, lax on terrorism, tax and spend liberal, the race card, permissiveness, was just too durable, and politically self-serving, and could always be dragged out to punch emotional hot buttons and sully the name and reputation of a political opponent. Obama was the biggest political threat the GOP had faced in a decade. This guaranteed that he'd get the full treatment of name calling. Socialist would be the perennial slur of record for him.

CHAPTER 6

The GOP Counterinsurgency

A Republican National Committee ad run in October 2004 called Democratic presidential contender John Kerry "the most liberal man in the Senate." Bush and GOP strategists pilloried Kerry as yet another tax and spend, pro abortion, pro gay rights, weak on national security, Democrat who was out of step with mainstream America.

Kerry did not have the most liberal voting record. He ranked at the bottom of the top 10 of Democratic senators in other surveys. But the ploy worked. In the waning days of the 2004 campaign, Kerry became in the minds of many voters the poster candidate for liberalism, and it was meant as a smear word. GOP strategists had the same template ready for the 2008 campaign. They quickly latched onto a terribly flawed February 2008 survey by the *National Journal* that ranked Democratic presidential contender Obama as the most liberal Senator in 2007.

He was not the most liberal senator either. He ranked at the bottom end of the top ten of Democratic senators. No matter, the L word slam was ancient and flawed, but still highly politically serviceable to tar a Democratic presidential candidate or even better a Democratic president. Thomas Dewey slapped the L word on Democrat Harry Truman. Dwight Eisenhower slapped it on Adlai Stevenson twice. Richard Nixon slapped it on JFK and Hubert Humphrey and George McGovern. Ronald Reagan slapped it on Walter Mondale twice. Bush Sr. slapped it on George Dukakis and tried to slap it on Bill Clinton. Bush Jr. slapped it on Al Gore and, of course, Kerry.

Over the years, the L word tact has been honed, massaged, tweaked and sprinkled with add-ons. Soft on communism, morphed into soft on terrorism, lax on permissiveness and law and order, was retooled as lax on crime. The add ons are that the Democratic candidates flip flop, are wishy washy, and will be weak commander in chiefs. Slander labels stoke emotions and passions, and stir visceral fears and beliefs. The GOP masterfully turned liberalism into a dread word and a dread fear for many voters. The absolute master at stoking the widespread suspicion and fear of liberalism and liberals to hammer Democrats was Ronald Reagan. An ebullient Regan blistered Democratic presidential nominee Michael S. Dukakis before a bulging crowd and a national television audience at the Republican National Convention in New Orleans in 1988 as the "liberal, liberal, liberal" whose policies were out of step with the American public. The line brought the house down, and during the ensuing campaign Dukakis was hopelessly tainted as the left wing candidate.

Though Obama wasn't the most liberal senator, his relatively liberal voting record on pet liberal issues gave the GOP its opening. It was only one opening. Another was to feed suspicions about his birth. That is that he was not a citizen, but an illegal alien, and had no legal right to run for the presidency, let alone be the president.

In July 2009, White House Press Secretary Robert Gibbs bluntly said that those adamant that he was an illegal alien and should be dumped from the White House would never go away. Not only wouldn't they go away but the "birthers" the nickname the press bestowed on them during the first part of 2009 gained even more steam. They gained it ironically with the unintended help of their opponents. Every newspaper, magazine, and talk show host that damned the birthers as a bunch of wacky, paranoid, Obama haters stirred the pot even more. They did it simply by acknowledging the issue with a column or a TV show. The birthers reveled in that. There was a canny, calculated and politically cynical motive behind the Obama birth certificate agitation.

The clamor for him to produce his original birth document gained a noisy following long before the final presidential vote tally was in November 2008. It started the instant he declared his presidential candidacy in February 2007. He was too black. He was not patriotic enough. He was too liberal, too effete, too untested. He was a Muslim, terrorist fellow traveler, and a closet black radical. The shock of Obama in the White House was simply too much for many to bear. He defied the stereotypical definition of what an American president was supposed to look like, and be like; namely a wooden image middle-aged, or older, white male.

He inadvertently gave ammunition to the incipient birthers during a campaign stop in late July 2007 when he quipped that he did not look like all those other presidents on the dollar bills. Obama got torched for saying the obvious and that was that his candidacy was different. He later admitted that it was a racial reference. The off the cuff remark simply reinforced the point that he and his candidacy marked a turning point in U.S. presidential politics and by extension race relations.

* * * * *

*T*he Obama birth certificate proponents kicked their rumor mongering campaign against him into even higher gear when some mainstream papers found the birth certificate controversy good copy and grist to get the tongues wagging. The birthers spotted the opening and crudely cloaked themselves in the mantle of public spirited citizens and legal experts with no personal, political, let alone racial ax to grind with Obama. They claimed that their sole goal was to insure electoral truth and accuracy, to make sure that all the legal requirements for holding a presidential office were met, and to head off a constitutional crisis. They even promised that they would put the matter to rest if he simply produced the original.

They didn't. The birthers got a subtle and at times open boost from GOP ultra conservatives. House Rep John Campbell and a dozen House GOP members for a time in the spring and summer of 2009 pushed a bill that required all future presidential candidates to produce their original birth certificates. That, of course, would apply to Obama when he presumably ran for reelection in 2012. In a debate on *MSNBC* in July 2009, Campbell was emphatic about his bill when he told indignant host Chris Matthews, "Wouldn't you like to put all this to rest? That's what this proposal is about." Though the majority of House Republicans in early August backed a resolution affirming Obama's Hawaiian birth, this by no means officially ended the GOP involvement in the movement to question Obama's Americanism. More than fifty Republicans didn't vote on the resolution.

The real value of the birther movement was that it was tailored to destabilize, or at least keep the Obama administration off balance on policy initiatives he was pushing on health care reform, the economy, and a softer foreign policy approach. Conservatives fiercely opposed him on all these counts.

Following Obama's inauguration in January 2009 dozens of You Tube clips were churned out on the controversy, droves of websites continued to recycle the rumor line about his certificate, and a mountainous size stack of articles rehashed the issue of whether the birth certificate that Hawaii produced was legitimate. More than two dozen lawsuits or petitions were filed in various state courts contesting his U.S. citizenship (one of them was filed by political gadfly Alan Keyes).

The Supreme Court's refusal in December 2008 to demand that he produce his birth certificate did absolutely nothing to take the wind out of the movement. If anything, it probably added to it by convincing more that the courts were in cahoots with the Obama White House to keep the real "truth" about his imagined foreign birth secret from the American people.

The worst thing about the controversy over his birth certificate was not that *CNN's* Lou Dobbs on several shows in July 2009 grabbed at the issue for ratings and to make mischief against Obama. Or that others in the media even dignified the controversy by treating it as if it was a legitimate issue. The worst thing was that few connected the dots to see the birthers as the shock troops to torpedo Obama's political agenda. Their hope was that by sowing enough conspiracy paranoia about him they could accomplish that. There was ample evidence that the campaign to taint his American citizenship had done exactly that. A *DailyKos/Research* 2000 poll found that nearly one quarter of Americans either didn't believe or weren't sure whether he was born in the United States. Even more telling, nearly sixty percent of Republicans either didn't believe he was an American citizen or had doubts about it.

* * * * *

*T*he birther movement was for most observers an amusing or disgusting sideshow. The far more lethal weapon in the anti-Obama attack arsenal was still America's oldest, deepest and touchiest issue, and that was race. It was the perennial brick and mortar marketing tool for the GOP, assorted hate groups and talk radio jocks. A Google search in August 2009 turned up more than three dozen active anti-Obama websites. Nearly all were filled with demeaning racist cartoons, depictions, characterizations and racially poisonous verbal bashes and attacks. As of mid-August, the sites had received more than 20 million Google search listed references.

The sheer weight and volume of the attacks slipped into the mainstream media. There were conservative *Fox TV Network* style racial quips, references and snipes from talk show hosts, guests, and commentators about Obama.

The vintage mix of race, anti-government politics, and top ratings was on near textbook display in the health care reform battle. In a rambling talk at the Conservative Political Action Conference on March 1, 2009, Rush Limbaugh strung words such as an unqualified Obama, liberal Democrats, a black guy, guilt, history, affirmative action, and liberal policies together. He covered all the racial rage bases and only mentioned race once.

In the midst of the furious debate over Obama's health care reform plan in the spring of 2009, the media played up the borderline racist attacks of Townhall health care town protestors as representative of a genuine, spontaneous grassroots campaign against health care reform, with no racial undertow. The fury of the anti-Obama protestors was so intense and race seemed to stick out as such an underlying motive behind their fury that an exasperated *New York Times* columnist Paul Krugman flatly said the prime motive of the protestors was racism. Syndicated columnist Cynthia Tucker went even further and put a percentage on the number of protestors that she called "racist." Her total was 45 to 65 percent.

Former House Republican Majority leader Dick Armey, however, paid no heed to percentages. His aim was to put bodies, lots of them, on Washington DC streets to oppose Obama's agenda. Led by a fife and drum corps, thousands of flag waving anti Obama protestors shook signs that read "Is this Russia?" "Traitors, Terrorists Run Our Government," and "Don't blame me I voted for The 'American'" trudged down Pennsylvania Avenue on September 12, 2009. The throng was a hodge podge of every group that had a beef against Obama, birthers, anti-abortionists, states righters and tax protestors.

* * * * *

Ahandful of top congressional Republicans at first expressed some leeriness over tying themselves too closely to the motley group of malcontents. Yet, the GOP couldn't deny the huge numbers and the real possibility of creating thousands of new shock troops in the movement to derail Obama's agenda, and to weaken the Democrats control of Congress in the 2010 midterm elections. The temptation was too great to pass up, "Could the Republican National Committee turn out 50,000 people on the mall," noted an effusive GOP strategist Craig Shirley. The Washington DC Fire Department actually put the figure at 70,000. That cinched it for GOP leaders. South Carolina Senator Jim DeMint, a featured speaker, thundered "Friends, this is a crucial battle for the heart and soul of America, for freedom itself." The star of the show though was the man who wasn't there. South Carolina congressman Joe Wilson who touched of a firestorm days earlier when he shouted out "you lie" during Obama's health care reform speech before a joint session of Congress was clearly the crowd hero. Many waved signs "We need more Joe Wilson's."

GOP leaders loudly protested any insinuation that racism fueled the taxpayer march, and indeed, all GOP opposition to Obama's agenda. They got a welcome boost from Obama. In interviews days after the march he flatly said that he did not see any overt or hidden racial animus behind the protests, and the continual verbal assaults from the right against him. Former President Jimmy Carter disagreed. A few days after the taxpayer march he told an *NBC* interviewer, "I think an overwhelming portion of the intensely demonstrated animosity toward President Obama is based on the fact that he is a black man, that he's an African-American."

Carter's outspoken candor brought a swift rebuke from House Democrats. They jumped over each other to assure that racism was not the engine driving the anti-Obama outbursts. Carter felt the heat from fellow Democrats and did a quick *mea culpa*. In a follow up interview he said that his remarks were "misinterpreted."

Racial hate and fear, however, clearly did drive more than a few to hit the barricades against Obama. But the drumbeat attacks on him were not done solely to shock, out of ignorance, to misinform, or to destabilize the Obama administration. There was a clear personal and political calculus to the race baiting. In the case of the shock jocks, the object was to cement their political influence, personal prestige, notoriety, and, of course, wealth. Hate groups use race to build bigger numbers, shake the money tree, and organize the gullible, hateful, and young.

The GOP had long subtly and at times crudely exploited racial fears to seize and expand its political dominance in all branches of the federal government, and in many states, especially the Deep South. Race baiting would not have worked if the GOP first during the Nixon years and later the Reagan years hadn't figured out that there were a lot of whites who were mad as hell at the feds for dumping a bloated, overblown big government on them. Lurking underneath their frustration was the finger point at minorities for the government bloat. This turned into the artful twist of hidden race animus into slogans such as "law and order," "crime in the streets," "welfare cheats," and "absentee fathers." President Bush's John Wayne frontier brashness, and get tough, bring em' on rhetoric in talking about Iraq and the war against terrorism was geared to appeal to supposed white male toughness.

The GOP also sensed something else that could make sneaky race tinged sloganeering and baiting work even better. Many blue collar white males were losing ground to minorities and women in the workplace, schools, and in society. The trend toward white male poverty and alienation actually first became evident in the early 1980s when nearly 10 million Americans were added to the poverty rolls and more than half were from white, male-headed families. Two decades later, the number of white men in poverty or among lower income wage earners continued to expand. The estimate was that more than one in five white males who voted in 2004 presidential election made less than $45,000 in household income.

The main culprit was always the big, intrusive federal government that tilted unfairly in spending priorities toward social programs that supposedly benefited minorities at the expense of hard working white males. That was exactly how hate groups, the anti-Obama web sites and bloggers, and talk jocks crafted the reason for the anger and alienation that many white males felt toward health care reform and by extension Obama. This of course translated into even more fear, rage and distrust of minorities.

* * * * *

By the end of the first year of his administration, the GOP counterinsurgency was in high gear against Obama. There were the familiar darts of race, liberal and socialist baiting, as well as his alleged foreign birth, and past radical associations aimed at him. There was another weapon that aided the assailers in inflicting damage. That was the White House's tactical stumble, and its gross underestimate of the potency of racial fears, hostility and paranoia. The stumble was to attack and keep attacking Rush Limbaugh and the shrill Obama antagonists. They totally dominate and abuse the airwaves. To pick a fight with them only inflated their importance, presence, and numbers.

His larger mistake was to misread the 2008 presidential election results. Much was made that he got more white votes than John Kerry or Al Gore; that he revved up young whites, and totally exorcised race from the campaign. Obama's win supposedly was final proof that America had finally kicked its racial syndrome. This was the stuff of media talk and wishful thinking. Despite a GOP racked by sex and corruption scandals, an anemic presidential opponent, a laughingstock vice presidential candidate, a collapsed economy and an outgoing GOP president with a rating worse than Herbert Hoover's, McCain still crushed Obama by a twelve point spread among white voters.

The route was not just among old, Deep South unreconstructed or latent bigoted white male voters, but in virtually every voter demographic among whites, including a narrow loss to Obama among a majority of younger white voters. This didn't tell the whole story of the sharp racial divide he faced. A sizeable percentage of whites were disgusted enough with Bush's policies to stay home on Election Day, but not disgusted enough with him and his policies to vote for Obama.

Obama's momentary defense of Harvard professor Henry Louis Gates after his altercation with a white Cambridge, Massachusetts police officer in July 2009 made more whites wary of Obama and his policies. The painful reality was that the crushing majority of whites, who opposed him or disavowed his policies for racial, party, or ideological reasons or personal prejudices, formed the backbone of the radical right's counter insurgency against him.

The GOP counterinsurgency would have taken flight no matter what he did. The party was still big, strong, well-positioned geographically, well-financed, and organized, and had its stock and time tested arsenal of weapons to bully, cajole and intimidate Democrats, especially liberal black Democrats, with. But the White House gave the counterinsurgency a generous boost with its fits and starts, and miscues on the economy, health care reform, and its shirk from taking the hard lead in confronting its congressional opponents. Former President Bill Clinton sensed that Obama was losing some momentum by not hitting back harder at the critics. In an interview in *Esquire Magazine* in early September 2009, Clinton bluntly told him to get tough with the Republicans, even write them off, "I wouldn't even worry about the Republicans. I'd worry about executing." Obama really didn't have much choice in the matter since the Republicans had made it abundantly clear that obstructionism and hostility would be their dual watchwords to anything he proposed. By the end of his first year, Obama hadn't lost the war against the GOP insurgents but there was no doubt that the insurgency would be a permanent and implacable force against him throughout his administration's first term.

CHAPTER 7

The Limbaugh Strawman

A few days after his inauguration President Obama met private-ly with congressional leaders to discuss his $1 trillion dollar stimulus plan. But Obama quickly digressed from the topic. He virtually ordered the Republicans at the meeting to tune out talk show kingpin Rush Limbaugh if they wanted to get things done with him.

The rebuke was understandable. Obama was in the first flush of his White House victory. He had won an electoral college land-slide victory. His popularity ratings were sky high, and he wanted and needed to get the stimulus package through Congress. The GOP was momentarily rocked back on its heels from their electoral trouncing. With his relentless on air assaults on Obama, Limbaugh seemed to be about the only real threatening voice among his detractors. The problem though was the attack, or rather the unintended consequence of Obama's attack. Limbaugh held no elected office, no GOP party position, and had no standing with the voters. He was a talk show jock. The attack inflated his importance even beyond the ratings popularity that he appeared to command. It made him a genuine and fearsome political player; a political strawman.

The unintended consequence of that was soon apparent. On March 2, 2009, Republican National Chair Michael Steele mildly chastised Limbaugh for his self-assigned dominant spot in the GOP. He got mountains of angry calls and letters for it. The next day a sheepish Steele called Limbaugh following his radio show and apologized. He sheepishly told an interviewer, ""My intent was not to go after Rush—I have enormous respect for Rush Limbaugh. I was maybe a little bit inarticulate. There was no attempt on my part to diminish his voice or his leadership." Steele's articulation was not in question, he had plenty of that on just about every radio and talk show that he could get a spot on. It was the fear of Limbaugh that made him do his *volte face* mea culpa.

Obama Chief of Staff, Rahm Emanuel, went one better than Obama or Steele. In an unsolicited remark on *CBS's Face the Nation* the day before Steele's apology, Emanuel lathered Limbaugh with both praise and scorn as the boss of the GOP. He called the brash talk show host the "voice and the intellectual force and energy behind the Republican Party."

Emanuel, as Obama, had an ulterior motive in anointing Limbaugh as White House Enemy Number 1. He was using him as a foil to tar the GOP as an antique, discredited, and obstructionist bunch of sore losers who would stop at nothing to derail Obama's policies. Steele was just simply running scared of Limbaugh.

All three did what Limbaugh couldn't do for himself and that was to wildly blow-up his importance as the GOP kingmaker. Limbaugh got the kind of promotion that ad companies spend millions on for nothing. But in the first couple of months of the Obama term it was still nothing but hot air. Limbaugh hadn't stopped one Obama staff or cabinet appointment, prevented one policy directive, executive order, or a single piece of legislation. That included Limbaugh's favorite target, Obama's economic stimulus bill. At that point, Limbaugh couldn't even stop his arch nemesis, Al Franken, from bagging the Minnesota senate seat. Franken's the guy who outrageously slammed Limbaugh as the big fat idiot, and then turned the slam into a best selling book.

Limbaugh's rambling, long winded, rant at the Conservative Political Action Conference in March 2009, punctuated by his confusion over what the Constitution and the Declaration of Independence say, was the topper. The crowd, which was heavily white and male, lapped up every Limbaugh inanity. A stroll through the convention hall showed that the crowd's divorce from political reality at that point was almost laughable. Every anti in America—taxes, gay rights, gun control, and government, as well as touting their darling Sarah Palin—was on display there. This appeared to further seal the GOP's lot as a party that was stepping fast toward becoming a self-marginalized, mean spirited, faded political entity. As events would soon show, it was way too early to write an obituary for the GOP, especially as long as Democrats were willing to commit the cardinal mistake of creating GOP strawmen out of jocks like Limbaugh and then watch with puzzlement and irritation as their prestige and popularity grew even bigger.

* * * * *

*T*his wasn't the first time that team Obama created and then punched away at a GOP strawman. When McCain plopped Palin on his ticket, a top Team Obama member reflexively hammered her. Obama quickly realized that it was a colossal mistake. He did the smart thing and simply congratulated her on being picked as McCain's VP candidate and then went back to talking about the issues. He knew not to make her the issue. The lesson didn't stick in the case of Limbaugh.

Making Limbaugh bigger than life in American politics gave steam to his inflammatory campaign of rumors, half truths, distortions, and flat out lies about Obama, liberals, and even RNC chief, Steele. Limbaugh's aim with Steele was to further cow the GOP into line; a line that formed behind him.

At the start of his tenure as RNC chair, Steele had the good sense to know that kowtowing to Limbaugh was a prescription for even bigger disaster for the GOP. He resuscitated the line that Bush used in 2000 on diversity and talked about making the GOP a party of big tent diversity. "We have been misdefined as a party that doesn't care, a party that's insensitive, a party that is unconcerned about minorities, a party that is unconcerned about the lives and the expectations and dreams of average Americans," Steele said. "Nothing could be further from the truth." Unfortunately, like Bush he promptly forgot his words.

This is exactly what Limbaugh with his conservative white man's litmus test for the GOP wanted. But this seemed to fly in the face of what Obama's election triumph showed. That was that the country's fast changing ethnic vote demographics looked nothing like it did as late as the presidential elections in the 1990s. In 2008, black, Hispanic, Asian and Native American voters made up nearly a quarter of the nation's electorate. College educated whites made up more than one-third of the vote. Limbaugh's comfort zone voter demographic; white blue collar, heartland and deep South voters had shrunk to less than forty percent of the nation's voters. Immigration, higher birth rates, and the youth trends could in future years swell the numbers of minority and youth voters even more.

It wasn't only the numbers that seemed to work against the GOP. It was also ideology. The Democrat's expanding core base of voters is more moderate, socially active, and pro government; the exact opposite of what Limbaugh rants for. Obama, Emanuel, and Steele know this. The Democrats would not have won the White House and Steele would not have beat out a pack of mostly Limbaugh fawning white contenders for the RNC top spot if that hadn't been true.

* * * * *

Politics, though, is never a straight line proposition. The picture was far more complex and nuanced than just growing numbers of ethnic minority voters and changing political demographics seemed to indicate. Limbaugh had one powerful tool to bully, badger and cajole the GOP and saber rattle Obama. That was the airwaves. He exploited it to the hilt. That didn't make him the boss of the GOP let alone any real threat to Obama. It just made him an inviting and convenient strawman.

The brutal reality for Obama and even the less doctrinaire GOP elected officials and supporters was that a narrow majority of GOP voters believed the party should think like Palin and be even more noisy and brutish in hectoring the GOP conciliators and of course, pounding Obama and the Democrats. In a radio broadcast in May 2009, he shoved back hard against any talk that the GOP should re-brand itself, "We did it their way in 2008. We did it with the candidate and approach that they thought would work. Now 'We got to listen to the American people.' I maintain that when a politician says we have to listen to the American people and learn, we are pandering. We're not leading."

Limbaugh well knew his audience and what they represented. It was overwhelmingly white, male and hard core conservative. This was and will remain the GOP's bread and butter constituency. They vote, are outspoken on issues, bully and badger Republican moderates and dissenters, and when fully aroused can inflame millions of voters around the emotional wedge issues; abortion, family values, anti-gay marriage and rights, and tax cuts.

It was fashionable after Obama's election to write off the GOP as an insular party of Deep South and narrow Heartland, rural and, non-college educated blue collar whites. This isn't a demographic to be totally sneered at, because the numbers are still huge. In fact, elections are uusually won by candidates with a solid and impassioned core of bloc voters. White males, particularly older white males, vote consistently and faithfully. And they vote in a far greater percentage than Hispanics and blacks.

GOP presidents and aspiring presidents, Nixon, Reagan, Bush Sr. and W. Bush, and McCain and legions of GOP governors, senators and congresspersons banked on these voters for victory and to seize and maintain regional and national political dominance. The strategy was simple; say and do as little as possible about civil rights, talk God, country and patriotism, use racially tinged code words and furiously court white males. The strategy worked like a political charm for four decades.

The strategy failed in 2008 only because of the rage and disgust of swells of white voters at Bush's horribly failed and flawed domestic and war policies. This was more a personal and visceral reaction to the bumbles of Bush than a radical and permanent sea change in overall white voter sentiment about Obama, the Democrats, and the GOP.

Limbaugh has never been shy about saber rattling the GOP and those within the party he considers GOP apostates. In January 2009, when Georgia rep Phil Gingrey had the temerity to accuse Limbaugh of taking holier than thou cheap shots at GOP congresspersons, Limbaugh quickly whipped up the talk show pack against him. Gingrey got the message to quickly change his tune and he did on none other than on Limbaugh's show, said an apologetic Gingrey "I clearly ended up putting my foot in my mouth on some of those comments (laughs) and I just wanted to tell you, Rush, and—and all our conservative giants who help us so much to maintain our base and grow it and get back this majority that I regret those stupid comments."

A gracious Limbaugh consoled Gingrey like a mother stroking a momentarily wayward son. Limbaugh was not presumptuous enough to take full credit for pumping steel in the back of GOP congresspersons to oppose much of the Obama economic stimulus bill, branding it another "pet liberal project." But he came close.

* * * * *

L imbaugh's total command of his airwave space gave him one of the most powerful weapons available to whip saw the GOP and saber rattle Obama. It was a formidable force to be reckoned with. The one time Federal Communications Commission Fairness Doctrine requirement that an offending station bring some semblance of balance to a discussion of an issue by the time Limbaugh hit the airwaves with force in the early 1990s was a faint memory.

Even when it was in play before Congress at Ronald Reagan's prodding in 1987 killed it did not drive a single conservative jock from the studio mics, diminish the power and profit of the syndicates, or chill free speech. It did just the opposite. The number of conservative talk radio hosts grew bigger, their influence greater, and the profits of corporate syndicates soared. In 1999, the five largest companies operated one out of five stations and generated nearly 50 percent of industry revenue. In 2006, they controlled more than one out of three stations and took in more than sixty percent of industry revenue.

Limbaugh hardly had sole possession of the airwaves weapon. Conservative talk radio has been a treasure chest of riches for the broadcast syndicates. Their talk jocks weld a power over millions that emperors, kings and dictators would kill for. A classic example of that was the debate over Obama's stimulus plan in the first two months of his term. There was some hint in the early days of the congressional debate over the plan that a few House Republicans might be willing to back the plan. Limbaugh and the conservative talking heads went to work and quickly changed that. They railed against it as a fatally flawed pork barrel laden, tax and spend, power grab scheme by Obama and the Democrats. This stiffened the spines of the GOP rank and file against the plan.

Once they had flexed their broadcast muscles and whipped the GOP back in line, the predictable next step was to browbeat any GOP dissenters on environment, immigration and particularly health care reform and any other major issue that conservative talk jocks deemed an Obama and Democratic Party power grab back into line. There was barely a peep of opposition let alone pro Obama administration support to be heard on the major talk radio airwaves.

The argument was made that by targeting Limbaugh, the best known and most popular GOP media voice, Obama, Emanuel and the Democrats could expose the political and intellectual dishonesty and ideological insularity and racial bigotry of many of those who made up the GOP leadership and its foot soldiers. The problem with this was that it also gave the GOP a bigger and wider platform to counter attack Obama and the Democrats with their patented charge that he was too liberal, too pro government, and too reckless in imposing runaway spending and crushing tax hikes. While Limbaugh seemed the perfect foil for the Democratic attack, he was also the perfect hero and rallying point for those who believed the worst about the Democrats.

Limbaugh for his part publicly tried to take the high road and stay above the fray. He sent an e-mail to the *Palm Beach Post's* Page 2 Live columnist Joe Lambiet a couple of days after Obama's January 2009 tongue lash of the House Republicans for bowing to him.

Limbaugh noted that, "The Great Unifier's plan is to isolate elected Republicans from their voters and supporters by making the argument about me and not about his plan. He is hoping that these Republicans will also publicly denounce me and thus marginalize me." In two terse sentences and despite the mock of Obama as the Great Unifier, Limbaugh managed to sound like an important, reasoned and level headed opponent of Obama's policies. This reconfirmed that he was a terrible pick for the Democrat's straw man.

CHAPTER 8

Obamacare: The Right or Wrong Prescription

*H*ealth and Human Services Secretary Kathleen Sebelius found out the hard way in July 2009 that when you say what your boss may really be thinking or worse end up doing on a crucial piece of legislation you quickly get smacked down. Sebelius in an unscripted and unvetted moment said that Obama's public option in the health care reform plan could go by the wayside if that's what it took to get his Senate opponents to back his reform bill. Sebelius didn't say anything that Obama's chief of staff, Rahm Emanuel hadn't insinuated weeks earlier, and that Obama himself suggested. The public option was not only expendable but at the top of the health reform endangered list.

Even if Sebelius, Emanuel, and Obama hadn't dropped the hint that it could be tossed, the public option plan drew almost no support from the key Senate Republicans and Democrats. Montana Democrat Max Baucus who was a major player in the health care reform fight, and chair of the Senate Finance Committee, did not include a public option plan in his health care reform proposal. In a leak in September 2009 strongly indicated that the negotiations within his committee over the plan did not include a public option. When Baucus unveiled his plan shortly after, as expected, it did not include a public option.

The short shrift that Baucus and other Senators gave to Obama's public option had much less to do with angry town hall protestors, the drum beat attacks from the *Fox News Network*, Limbaugh, and the pack of conservative bloggers, as well as the GOP orchestrated Senate attacks on the public option, than Obama the politician. Obama had sent guarded, and very mixed signals in the first few months of the health care reform debate about just how strongly he would mount the barricades against any effort to strip the bill of the public option.

At an AFL Labor Day picnic on September 8, 2009 at Coney Island in Cincinnati, he sent an ambiguous signal that he would back some from of a public option. He called it necessary but only as part of a "basket" of health care options. He openly tipped his hand on how he would deal with the public option in his make or break speech to Congress two nights later. The real issue was whether the president would fight for it. He sent off the same mixed signal in the speech. The public option was desirable, but it wasn't mandatory to get a final deal.

Obama dropped two other hints that he would not fight for the public option. The day after the speech House Speaker Nancy Pelosi, up to then a ferocious verbal backer of the public option changed her tune and said that she was flexible on it. The change came after a meeting at the White House. At the same time a frustrated and perturbed group of progressive congressional Democrats complained that Obama had reneged on a promised meeting with them. They wanted the meeting to press him to stand firm on the public option.

* * * * *

*O*bama needed to win a big victory on health care, or at least the appearance of a victory, even if the victory meant scrapping the only thing in the health care reform package that really represented true health care reform. He was not going to make the mistake that then President Bill Clinton did fifteen years earlier in January 1994 when he defiantly told a Joint Session of Congress that: "If you send me legislation that does not guarantee every American private health insurance that can never be taken away, you will force me to take this pen, veto the legislation, and we'll come right back here and start all over again." Clinton threw down the gauntlet to the GOP and then they promptly threw it back at him. House Republicans made sure that any health care reform bill that he sent to congress was DOA.

Yet, a government health insurance option was the only real lever to make the pharmaceuticals and health care insurers lower drug costs, reduce their astronomical profit rake offs, deliver better services, eliminate the endless dodges that insurers use to pick and choose only the most healthy and profitable patients, and make some dent in the 45 to 50 million uninsured. If private health insurers and the pharmaceuticals had made those reforms years earlier without a government lever, the whole health care debate and crisis would have long since been a moot point.

At the same time, Obama could not ignore the legitimate criticism of the plan he offered and the compromise senate plans. There were troubling questions aplenty. Where would the billions come from with the federal government facing massive and rising deficits to subsidize the poor, and uninsured poor that would be under mandate to purchase insurance from a private carrier? What safeguards were in place to insure that the pharmaceuticals reduced drug costs and kept them down? And what safeguards were there to insure that private carriers did not escalate insurance prices once the congressional and public spotlight was off the new health care law? And what enforcement mechanisms would be in place to prevent insurers from developing new ploys to dump those with pre-existing medical conditions? What iron clad cost containment measures were there to prevent the future costs of health care from ballooning out of control and further hiking the deficit?

The answers to the questions were hazy. This continued to open the door wide for conservatives and liberal Democrats to wage war against Obama's health care reform plan as either too costly and too intrusive or too tightfisted and too restricted. The questions and criticisms were virtual reruns of what Democratic presidents had faced during the past six decades in their fight to get comprehensive health care for Americans.

In 1945 when Harry Truman proposed national health care as part of his Fair Deal reform package the AMA immediately declared war. It branded it socialized medicine, and hired a pricey PR firm to launch media and public broadsides against the Truman plan. The US Chamber of Commerce churned out a pamphlet entitled "You and Socialized Medicine." When public approval of the plan plummeted faster than a cast iron anchor, the plan was effectively dead.

The AMA beat the war drums against JFK in 1961 when he set up a commission to study the possibility of a government insurance program for the elderly and disabled. The man that pounded the drum the hardest for the AMA was then actor Ronald Reagan. Reagan cut a record for the AMA denouncing what later became Medicare as "a short step to socialism." The furious attack was just as loud when Lyndon Johnson actually proposed the Medicare plan. Opponents used the same template that they used against Truman and Kennedy, a pricey PR firm, high priced lobbyists, and the scare tactic of socialized medicine. It didn't work with LBJ. He had the political skills, ruthlessness, connections, the liberal reform spirit of the civil rights movement, and a prosperous pre -Vietnam War economy behind him.

He got his way and Medicare became a fact of American life. This was the last Democratic presidential victory over the powerful pharmaceuticals, major health insurers, and medical establishment. Bill and Hillary Clinton got the full socialized medicine scare treatment with their health care reform plan in 1994. It included a massive media and letter writing campaign by small business owners, wildly sensationalist ads, and seminars around the country. The Clintons soon threw in the towel on their plan.

* * * * *

*T*here was one other major issue that stymied health care reform for decades beyond simply the arguments about high costs, government intrusion, and alleged subversion of medical and individual freedom. That was the fear by hospitals, insurers and medical personnel of having to cover and treat the millions of largely poor black and Hispanics with no insurance and no means to pay. The Commonwealth Fund in a report in April 2007 found that blacks and Hispanics made up nearly half of the estimated 45 to 50 million Americans that had no health care insurance. They were far more likely than the one in four uninsured whites to experience problems getting treatment at a hospital or clinic, and to have fewer if any choices in getting health care coverage.

The gaping racial disparity in the number of uninsured was the big sticking point for any Democratic president that talked about a national health care plan. The disparity in the access to and quality of health care for minorities fueled much of the crisis and the urgency for reform. Countless studies have shown that blacks and Hispanics suffer higher rates of catastrophic illnesses and diseases, are much less likely to obtain basic drugs, tests and preventive screening, to be admitted to hospitals and to have surgery. They are more likely to recover slower from illness, and they die much younger.

Studies have found that when blacks and Hispanics do receive treatment, the care they receive is more likely to be substandard to that of whites. Studies have found that even when blacks and Hispanics are enrolled in high quality health plans the care and quality of medical treatment gaps still remain.

Private insurers selectively pick the best and most well-endowed patients financially to bloat profits and hold down costs. American medical providers spend twice as much per person than providers in countries that provide universal health care, and provide less quality for the inflated bucks. Insurers get a rake off on both ends. Patients pay more in higher insurance premiums, co payments fees and a grab bag of other hidden health costs. At the same time, government medical insured programs also shell out more than public insurers in other countries with universal health care.

The massive public attention and anger over the health crisis caused insurers, their lobbyists and political flacks to scramble. The America's Health Insurance Plans, the major insurer industry group, announced in July 2009 that it would put its considerable muscle behind health care reform. On the surface, the announcement seemed to be a major breakthrough in that the industry had finally seen the light and would work hand in hand with Obama to make real health care reform a reality. The group had softened its resistance to providing coverage to those that it labeled "high risk" or less charitably, "undesirables." That's the millions who suffer chronic and major diseases—cancer, diabetes, asthma and heart disease. Blacks and Latinos have higher incidences of these ailments than whites.

The change came only after guarantees were made that the government would subsidize the cost of covering high risk cases. Even that concession was suspect. The issue was still cost and the standard fear of private insurers of government control of medical care. Private insurers and their lobbyists repeatedly cited that as their reason for scuttling health care reforms. Obama's mere mention that he'd impose higher taxes on the wealthy to pay for coverage of the uninsured stirred anxiety among some insurers and medical industry groups of deficit soaring taxes and socialized medicine.

The sweetener for private insurers was that the government would mandate that everyone buy insurance under the threat of penalty. This was a giant giveaway to the insurers, and guaranteed a vast new pool of clients, many of whom would be bought and paid for by taxpayer dollars. It was the only way that industry groups and insurers would sign on and end their age old battle against reform.

But just when the White House's assumed pact with the private insurers seemed a done deal, they tossed Obama a curve. On the eve of the vote by the Senate Finance Committee to approve the watered down reform plan the private insurers were in apparent agreement on, the AHIP fired off to the press the result of a study it commissioned that claimed that the health care reform plan would hike the cost of insurance for families by thousands. The study insisted that private employers would get hit even harder with the increased fees, taxes, and add-on costs in the reform plan and that would cause many employers to reduce or even eliminate coverage for employees. It was blackmail pure and simple, especially after the group threatened to spend a fortune on an ad campaign against Obama's plan. The White House quickly dismissed the study as such. But it was yet another reminder of the vehemence of private insurer's opposition to yielding any of their traditional dominance and control on health care.

The battle for universal health care was a titanic struggle between a health care industry that had its way for six decades and gutted every proposal and plan for expanded health care. The arguments were the same again—-cost, inefficiency, heavy handed government control and interference. Race, of course, was never mentioned as a reason to water down or shelve completely his reform plan. But it lurked underneath. Even that reason could be brushed aside if the price and profits for insurers and health care providers in reform was right.

* * * * *

*T*here was much speculation and debate about whether Obama would or even should sign the final health reform bill when it was delivered to his desk without a public option feature. There was little doubt what he'd do. He'd sign the bill. He simply had too much political and personal capital invested in it not to. He would declare it the greatest victory for health care reform since LBJ inked Medicare into law four decades ago. Politically, though it would still leave many dissatisfied. Conservatives would still scream that it was a step down the road to socialized medicine. Progressives would still scream that it did too little to insure the millions of uninsured have affordable, quality medical care, and provide any real watchdog check on the major pharmaceticals to make sure they dropped the costs, and kept them dropped on prescription drugs.

The bill was in reality a patchwork compromise bill with many uneven parts. But legislative compromise had become Obama's special forte. A presidential campaign, a White House win, and a presidency that relied firmly on bipartisanship, had drastically changed the political game and Obama. He had to appease many factions, and the most important were the Republican senators that he would have to do some business with to get key legislation passed.

Many Democrats implored him to stop trying to placate the Republicans in trying to pass his health care reform plan. Republicans accused him of forging ahead without them in trying to ram his health care agenda through congress. The fact remained that Obama never stopped trying to get some GOP support, as hopeless as it seemed, for a health care reform deal. He effusively praised McCain, and other GOP senators in his health care reform speech beforce Congress in September 2009. The back pedal, shifts, and concessions to the GOP to get a final health care reform bill into law was just another example of how business on Capitol Hill gets done.

CHAPTER 9

Obama's Racial Trainwreck

*T*he question *Chicago Sun Times* columnist and Washington Bureau chief correspondent Lynn Sweet posed to President Obama at his press conference in July 2009 seemed innocuous enough, "Mr. President, What does that incident say to you? And what does it say about race relations in America?" The incident was Cambridge Police Sgt. James Crawley cuff and arrest of Harvard Professor Henry Louis Gates on the front porch of Gates' home.

Sweet later took great pains in interviews and in her column to explain that the question was not a plant, or a set-up, and certainly not part of a conspiracy to embarrass Obama. In fact, Sweet protested that she would have asked the exact same question of former President Bush. But the question hit on the one issue, namely race that the president spent virtually an entire presidential campaign, and his first months in the White House, saying virtually nothing on. Little did Sweet know or expect that the short question would ignite a firestorm of howls and rage, volumes of TV and talk radio chatter and, a furious internet buzz that quickly lapped at the heels of Obama. His off-the cuff quip calling the cuffing and arrest by Crawley "acting stupid" did just that.

A shell shocked Obama quickly backed off from his knock of the officer in a follow-up interview. He made it clear that he wasn't indicting the entire Cambridge police department. By then the damage had been done. Two presidential approval polls from *Rasmussen* and *Zogby* confirmed the nightmare from the fallout. The *Rasmussen* poll was an absolute number's nightmare for Obama. His disapproval rating soared to nearly 40 percent among voters. Those who strongly approved of his performance sunk to less than 30 percent. This wasn't the worst of the bad news. A bare 25 percent of voters thought his answer was good. More than 60 sixty percent thought it was fair or lousy. Even more ominous was the voter breakdown. The crack in Obama's hitherto impregnable black vote support was glaring. Nearly 30 percent of black voters broke ranks with Obama on his Gates' answer, and questioned his response and even the fact that he made one at all.

Among Obama's two other huge breakthrough groups, independents, and young voters, the blowback was even more disastrous. Nearly 70 percent of Independents and nearly 50 percent of young persons rated his answer "fair" or "poor." The Gates affair gave his opponents another opening to blast the president, and by extension his policies on health care, the stimulus, and on foreign policy overtures. All were suddenly back in play and in question as set hit pieces for his critics; but especially health care reform. The issue was no longer the standard knock that it was too costly and a gross case of too much government interference in health care. Obama had now become too many an anti-police and an out of the closet race baiter.

The more charitable didn't go that far, but instead firmly declared that the presidential honeymoon was officially over. The only good news was that Obama's popularity outside the U.S. was still high. However, foreigners can't vote for or elect the US congresspersons and senators who make and decide major policy decisions.

He spoke from the heart and said what needed to be said about the thorny issue of race and especially racial profiling for which he really need not have apologized. However, the Gates flap was a racial train wreck waiting to happen.

* * * * *

*T*his was the last thing that Obama wanted or needed to happen. He had taken every possible pain and precaution to insure that race was kept off the campaign table and his embryonic presidency's table. During the campaign Republican presidential rival McCain was dead on point about the role race played in the campaign. In an interview the last week of the campaign in October, he told *CNN's* Larry King that he didn't think race would be much of an issue in the final vote. As McCain put it only "a tiny, tiny, minority" would vote against Obama because he was black. This was not just McCain campaign puffery to tout his credential as a play it straight on race guy. Race was never the factor in the campaign that many thought and some hoped that it would be. Obama took it off the table with his race neutral pitch and appeal on the issues. He made sure it stayed off the table.

More than 100 days into the President's term he made doubly sure that it stayed that way. In February 2009 Attorney General Holder lambasted Americans for being cowards in not talking about and dealing with race. Obama, in a mild rebuke of Holder at a press conference, softened the tone and reminded that racial confrontation is not his style or his way. In another press conference, he shrugged off a question about race by simply saying that any racial back patting about his election "lasted about a day".

His relative silence on racial matters did much to continue to shove the always volatile issue to the nation's backburner. This was amply confirmed in an April 2009 *New York Times/CBS* poll. It found that Americans by large margins said that race relations were good, and more blacks than ever said the same.

McCain and Obama's best efforts to make race a non-issue in the campaign and his race neutral approach to policy making and statecraft, however, would have fallen short without the sea change shift in public attitudes. The decade since the Rodney King beating in 1991, the O.J. Simpson trial in 1995, and the urban riots in 1992 that followed the acquittal of the LAPD officers that beat King, has been a period of relative racial peace in America.

During that time polls consistently showed that more whites than ever were genuinely convinced that America is a color-blind society, equal opportunity is a reality, and blacks and whites if not exactly attaining complete social and economic equality, are closer than ever to that goal. Though the figures on income, education and health care still show a colossal gap between poor blacks and whites, the perception nonetheless is that racism is an ugly and nasty by-product of a long by-gone past.

At times during the campaign Obama was asked whether he would back special initiatives and programs to deal with the racial disparities that still ensnare millions of poor blacks and Latinos. His answer was always to acknowledge that the inequities exist. But the best way to attack them was with more and new programs and greater spending on housing, education, and job creation, as well as tougher enforcement of civil rights and voting rights laws. It was a variation on the old "rising tide lifts all ships" approach to solving the problems of the poor, and since the ships that are in the poorest shape of all are those of the poor and minorities, they would benefit the most by this approach. And any stand alone talk about race just muddied things up.

His diffusing race was not to deny that racial problems exist and still corrode much of American society. It was just simply good and smart politics, and for a black man treading into the uncharted territory for blacks of presidential politics it was also safe politics. In a weekend of network TV interviews in late September 2009 to push his health care reform plan, he was constantly asked about race, and whether it was the reason for the intense opposition to his agenda and him. Obama again shrugged off race as the motivating force behind the opposition.

* * * * *

Better than any other presidential candidate, Obama understood that excessive talk of civil rights has been taboo in all recent America presidential races. It seeped into presidential debates only when a Democratic or Republican presidential contender or president snatched at the issue to assure middle class voters that he would not tilt toward or pander to minorities or to race bait their opponents.

In a 1988 debate, Bush Sr. slammed Democratic contender Michael Dukakis as being soft on crime for allegedly letting black convict Willie Horton roam free to commit rape and murder. Bill Clinton used Jesse Jackson as a prop to assure middle class voters that he would fight just as hard as conservative Republicans to protect their interests. In one of their debates in 2000, Bush and Democratic rival Al Gore clashed over affirmative action. Both were intent to distance themselves from the issue.

Obama knew that talk of civil rights invariably translates out to talk of race. This was a minefield that could blow up at any time and the explosion could mortally wound his candidacy. The endless TV sound loop of his former pastor Jeremiah Wright's inflammatory racial tirades in the midst of his fierce primary battle with Hillary Clinton sent momentary shocks through the campaign. It forced him to scramble fast and do damage control. The Wright flap guaranteed that race would not be even a vague utterance during the remainder of the campaign.

The hard racial lines in Obama's victory also sobered him to the minefield of race. He obliquely alluded to it in his thank you victory speech in Chicago's Grant Park on Election Night when he said that he was well aware that many people did not support him but he promised to work hard to win their support. This plainly disap-pointed some black Democrats who quietly and occasionally publicly urged the president to say more about racial issues. That simply was not in the White House cards.

"I feel responsibility and obligation to serve the president and the nation and black people certainly are part of this county," said Cassandra Butts, deputy White House counsel, "The issues we work on certainly have an impact on the African-American community, but the black staff isn't having a conversation every day to figure out how to serve black people."

* * * * *

*O*bama's hyper caution on race was politically wise and neces-sary for another reason. He never had anything resembling the big, popular mandate that the press and Democrats believed he had among whites to make sweeping change. The sign of that was literally evident in some of the overt racially inflammatory signs waved on September 12, 2009, by many of the taxpayer marchers that shuffled down Pennsylvania Avenue. They read: "The Long Legged Mack Daddy," "Where's the Birth Certificate," "Mississippi Freedom Riders," "Whoa Boys Take it from Here" (Obama waving to black and Islamic militants). Many defiantly waved the Confederate flags, and the Texas state flag (separatist movement emblem).

Meanwhile, South Carolina senator Jim DeMint, congressper-sons Mike Pence, Phil Gingrey and Marsha Blackburn, and organiz-er mouthpiece scandal plagued former House majority leader Dick Armey profusely swore that the march had nothing to do with race, politics, or even President Obama. The racist flags, symbols and signs, though, made their claim that race was not a factor in the loathe of Obama by many tax protestors disingenuous at best, and an untruth at worst. Racism was on full and ugly display on the Capitol Mall. No attempt was made to mask it. Some protestors seemed quite proud to openly send a message about race and Obama.

DeMint and Armey's public pretense that the Taxpayer March was non-partisan, with absolutely no racial overtone or anti-Obama motive to it was the stock ruse to play the race card while disavowing any play of it. The GOP has honed the ruse to a science the past four decades.

During the Nixon years and later during the Reagan years, GOP leaders figured that there were a lot of white guys out there who were mad as hell at the feds for dumping a bloated, overblown big government on them. Underneath their frustration was the finger point at minorities for the government bloat. That turned into the artful twist of hidden race animus into slogans such as "law and order," "crime in the streets," "welfare cheats," and "absentee fathers." These were all carefully crafted to punch the anger and frustration of many whites at blacks without getting the muck of racism on their hands.

The GOP also sensed that racial sloganeering and race baiting could work by playing on the false fear of blue collar white males that they were losing ground to minorities and women in the workplace, schools, and in society. The main culprit was always the big, intrusive federal government that leaned unfairly in spending priorities toward social programs that benefited minorities at the expense of hard working white males. This translated out to even more fear, rage and distrust of minorities. The venerable blend of race and anti-government politics was on textbook display often in the health care reform battle.

The racial assault by droves of taxpayer marchers was simply the latest in the racial pillorying of Obama. There were dozens of active anti-Obama websites. All were stuffed with demeaning racist cartoons, depictions, characterizations and racially poisonous verbal bashes and attacks against him.

It was perhaps fitting that many taxpayer marchers turned South Carolina congressman Joe Wilson into a near mythical folk hero. He was the congressman who shouted "you lie" at Obama during his joint congressional speech on health care reform five days prior to the march. There were buttons and banners backslapping Wilson for hitting back at Obama. Long before Wilson's blasphemous outburst at Obama during his congressional speech on health care reform he cut his teeth battling hard to beat back the NAACP challenge to remove the Confederate flag from its long standing perch at the front of the South Carolina state capitol building.

Wilson's battle to preserve as he proudly noted the flag that typifies "our heritage" was par for the course for GOP racist tinged politics in South Carolina. Wilson swam squarely in the mainstream of that brand of race politics with other GOP politicians in the state. On September 12, he had good company with legions of taxpayer marchers.

* * * * *

*W*hile presidential candidate Obama had to observe the rules of political expediency to win and establish a firm foothold on the White House, there was some pressure to say and do something about racial ills, mostly because they hadn't magically disappeared with his election. In its annual State of Black America reports during the first decade of 2000, the National Urban League repeatedly warned that blacks were less likely to own their own homes, are more likely to die earlier, are far more likely to be jailed disproportionately and receive longer sentences, receive less or poorer quality health care and earn far less than whites. The poor largely attend failing public schools, and were more likely the victims of racially motivated hate crimes than any other group.

The report also found rampant discrimination and gaping economic disparities between Latinos and whites. In the past decade, the income, and education performance gaps between blacks and Latinos and whites have only marginally closed, or actually widened. Discrimination remained the major cause of the disparities. Shunting civil rights to the back burner of presidential campaigns almost always meant that once in office presidents shunted them to the backburner of their legislative agenda.

Yet, presidents have not been able to totally tap dance around racial problems. Reagan's administration was embroiled in affirmative action battles. Bush Sr.'s administration was tormented by urban riots following the beating of black motorist Rodney King. Clinton's administration was burdened with conflicts over affirmative action, police violence and racial profiling. W. Bush's administration was confronted by the HIV/AIDS pandemic, voting rights, reparations, and affirmative action battles, gang violence, and failing inner city public schools. By ignoring, or downplaying these issues until they burst into flashpoints of national debate and conflict, presidents have been ill prepared to craft meaningful legislation and programs to deal with them.

In any case, civil rights and the ramp up in spending on education, housing and jobs, and health care programs have not been a priority for presidents in the past half century. Lyndon Johnson was the sole exception. That was only because of relentless pressure from the civil rights movement and the urban violence that tore apart America.

In the first days of his administration, Obama listed "Civil Rights" as the first item under his "Agenda" on his White House website, whitehouse.gov. He pledged to end gender and race based pay disparities, push through the Fair Pay and Employment Non-Discrimination Acts, harshly penalize voter fraud, outlaw racial profiling by federal law enforcement agencies, provide financial incentives to local and state police to ban racial profiling, and to dump the race tinged drug sentencing disparities. He also promised to push through Congress the long stalled Matthew Shepard Act. This markedly expands hate crime prosecutions.

The real test was whether he would move civil rights from agenda items on the White House website to a vigorous and active fight to enact them into law.

The gnawing problem that he had in trying or even being perceived as an activist president on civil rights was the problem that bedeviled all moderate Democratic presidents. That's because to make even the most tepid pronouncements on increased civil rights protections was instantly pounced on by conservatives as favoring minorities at the expense of whites. As president and an African-American, this was an even heavier burden that Obama was forced to bear.

CHAPTER 10

Obama's Afghanistan Nightmare

*S*enator Barack Obama was hot on the presidential campaign trail in August 2007 when he made an impassioned pledge at the Woodrow Wilson International Center for Scholars, "When I am president I will wage the war that has to be won." That war was the war in Afghanistan. He promised to quickly get out of Iraq, corral America's allies in a partnership to wipe out the terrorists and their mass destructive weapons, end corruption in the government, hold free elections, and insure a stable government in Afghanistan.

Obama, however, left no doubt that he strongly believed the key to making this happen was stability in the country and that could only come through U.S. battlefield victories. This meant more troops, weapons and fighting. He said that he would immediately deploy two more troop brigades to the country, mostly recycled troops from an Iraq war wind down, and plough $1 billion more to fund the added troop build-up. This was a charitable underestimate of what it would take to get stability and to turn the military battle tide.

Two years after candidate Obama's promise to up the U.S. military ante in Afghanistan and a shell out of $230 billion dollars, and more than 700 US dead, not one of these goals had been met, least of all corruption free, democratic elections. Yet, he still demanded more money, $65 billion in August 2009, for troop and infrastructure build-up in the country with little guarantee that the added money would attain any better results. Ironically, the $65 billion was an amount bigger than the amount budgeted for Iraq at the time; and the 17,000 more troops would bring troop deployment in Afghanistan close to the number in Iraq.

A Pentagon plan for 45,000 troops by the end of 2009 would top the number of American troops in Iraq at its peak. There still was no guarantee that Obama would be any closer to attaining the goal of severely crippling Al Qaeda and installing a corruption free, democratic government there after the build-up.

Military analysts, Pentagon insiders, and the Joints Chiefs, agreed that to achieve anything faintly close to Obama's goals in Afghanistan would take a long hard slog that would cost billions more and take thousands more American troops (with increased casualties). In an *MSNBC* interview in April 2009, former Secretary of State Colin Powell applauded Obama's determination to see the war through to an end in Afghanistan.

But he also cautioned that more troops, more money, and the

eternal struggle to implant a stable, pro-US government weren't enough. "I think ultimately it ends up with America, NATO and the UN all coming together to help the Afghans put together a security force that can provide security for the country so that it isn't going to take American troops and NATO forever to be there and, if that can be the case, that we have security forces built up to the point where they can manage security and a government that's functioning and that has control throughout the country. That would be a success."

By the end of 2009, the Taliban was back and stronger than ever in Eastern Afghanistan. The success that Powell sought seemed more and more like a forlorn hope.

* * * * *

A ghanistan was a difficult war to wage let alone win for reasons that went beyond simply finding a democratic government and pouring more US troops into the country and shoring up a stable, corruption free governnment. It blended religious fanaticism, medieval beliefs, territorial imperative, and deeply flawed political assumptions about terrorism into a nightmare cauldron. Afghans, whether fighting the British a century ago and later the Russians, waged the wars spurred by a rigid, uncompromising Islamic fundamentalism that reached way beyond the tenets of traditional Islam. God was always on their side. Even if there were any validity to the fantasy notion that Afghanistan could be cleared of the Taliban by military action alone, that would hardly end the threat of terrorist attacks. Terrorist groups could easily regroup in a host of other safe havens in places such as Somalia, Yemen, Indonesia, the Sudan,

Lebanon, and Iran and continue to receive financial backing through drugs, illicit arms sales, and covert state government backing. Then there were the terror targets themselves.

A study of suicide attacks by Robert Pape of the Chicago Project in 2005, found that almost all terror attacks and targets are aimed at getting the occupying forces to pull their troops out of a disputed territory whether it's Iraq, the West Bank, Israel, or Afghanistan. A bigger US occupation far from diminishing the prospect of more terror attacks assures that there will be more of them with US forces being in the terrorist bulls eye.

Military analysts were genuinely surprised in 2009 that the massive US build-up hadn't achieved the goal of reducing the influence and numbers of Taliban fighters and supporters within Afghanistan and Pakistan and by extension diminishing the threat of more terror attacks. Yet, there was a direct inverse correlation between the military ramp up in rural areas and the ramp up in support for the radicals. The obvious conclusion was that the thousands more US troops would stir even greater resistance.

Local army operations in the rural areas to obliterate entire villages in collective punishment, and cross-border raids by US forces and Hellfire missile attacks from Predator drones that often mistakenly hit civilian targets were the greatest recruitment aids for the Taliban and terrorist groups. The US, European and Asian allies were clearly seen by huge numbers of Afghans not as liberators and friends but as oppressors and foes. 50,000 more troops and billions more US dollars just meant 50,000 more enemies, and a massive drain of dollars that accomplished little to make the discredited Afghan government any more credible. The war on terror fought in Afghanistan then could easily feed itself for years with a generous supply of US military fodder.

* * * * *

*T*he battle over means and ends in Afghanistan touched off a brief behind the scenes tussle between Obama and the Pentagon when General Stanley McChrystal said that the US should deploy up to 45,000 more troops in the country by the end of September 2009. That would nearly double the 62,000 troops that were there in August 2009. This was clearly a troop number that Obama was uncomfortable with. This had less to do with any wavering of his commitment to win the war. From his early speeches before taking office Obama remained doggedly convinced that the Afghan war could be won, no matter the cost. And he was willing to stake the credibility of his administration on that, no matter the price.

In an August 2009 speech to the Veterans of Foreign Wars at their convention, Obama sounded the same theme that winning the Afghanistan war was the frontline defense against international terrorism. "This is not a war of choice. "This is a war of necessity. Those who attacked America on 9/11 are plotting to do so again. If left unchecked, the Taliban insurgency will mean an even larger safe haven from which Al Qaeda would plot to kill more Americans."

His slight push back in September 2009 against the massive troop deployment had everything to do with politics. The same month Vice President Joe Biden had given him an alternate scenario and that was to scale back the troop commitment in Afghanistan and concentrate on targeted attacks against Al Qaeda wherever it was found. This made the timing even worse for him to agree to a Pentagon request for a huge leap in American troops as well as a huge bump up in dollars to pay for the build-up.

A mid-August 2009 *Washington Post-ABC News* poll confirmed that. It found that more Americans than ever said the war was pure folly. A majority of Obama's most fervent backers said the same. These were the supporters who Obama would need to beat back the mounting GOP counterinsurgency against him that had steadily gained momentum through the middle of 2009, make gains or at least cut potential Democratic losses in the mid-term elections in 2010, and to vigorously pump his shaky health care reform package. In mid-September the grumbles from liberal Democrats and progressives were louder about his perceived backslide on many of his campaign promises. But the word that Obama heard more of and troubled him most was Vietnam. This is the universal symbol of a war that shouldn't have been fought and couldn't be won. In other words it stood for a military and political quagmire.

He was well aware of the Vietnam War comparison. At a White House dinner with a group of the nation's leading historians, there was talk about the pitfall of turning Afghanistan into a Vietnam type muddle and how this could seriously derail his administration's agenda on domestic and other foreign policy matters. Robert Caro, LBJ's biographer, was at the dinner and noted that Johnson had made many of his ill-fate decisions about Vietnam at the same dining table where Obama, Caro and his other historian guests sat. "All I could think of when I was sitting there and this subject (Vietnam) came up was the setting," Caro said. "You had such an awareness of how things can go wrong." While he wouldn't say what Obama said about the Vietnam-Afghanistan analogy and the parallel with what John-son faced, he did admit that Obama had a broad understanding of history and knew the peril it could pose to his administration's suc-cess.

The Vietnam-Afghanistan analogy, though, was not an exact parallel. The Vietnam war spanned three presidencies, involved half million US ground troops, resulted in more than 50,000 US war dead, was a tail end spin off of the Cold War. It involved a big power face off between the US and China and the Soviet Union. The Vietnam War was in the end a clash between a fiercely entrenched nationalist movement fighting to shed decades of colonial rule and a US govern-ment still profoundly discolored by Cold War big power paranoia.

Yet, Obama's Vietnam-Afghan fear was not an overblown fear.

* * * * *

An exultant George Bush Sr. at the end of the US route of Sad-dam Hussein in the Gulf War in 1991 declared "By God we've finally kicked the Vietnam syndrome." The president's exult was premature to say the least. Vietnam was still the dreaded word that Presidents Johnson, Clinton, and W. Bush heard about Vietnam, Somalia, and Iraq. A comparison of recent US wars fought to Viet-nam has been a political negative for presidents. These wars soured public opinion, drained the economy, fueled public dismay and an-ger, hampered passage of their domestic programs, fractured their party, and stirred big losses in Congress.

Public shell shock over unpopular wars always redounds to the advantage of an incumbent challenging a president whose name is linked to the war. In 1952, Eisenhower ran on the pledge to visit Korea if elected. Though Ike never directly promised to bring the troops home if elected, the implicit commitment was that if elected he'd do that. He really didn't have to make that promise; public weariness over the war was so great that Ike's generic oath to visit the troops was enough to help sink Truman. In the public's mind the Korean War had become Truman's war, or more accurately Truman's failure to win the war.

Similarly, Nixon learned from Ike. During the presidential campaign against Democratic Vice-President Hubert Humphrey in 1968, Nixon dropped careful politically calculated hints of a "secret plan" to end the Vietnam War if elected. Like Ike, he didn't spell out in any real detail just what his secret plan was. And like Ike, he didn't really have to. Public revulsion over Vietnam, as in Korea, was so great that even the scintilla of a suggestion that Nixon could end the war aroused voter optimism for him and even greater fury against Humphrey who was widely seen as the caretaker of Johnson's war (Johnson saw the handwriting on the wall and declined to run).

These two unpopular wars helped do in Truman and the Democrats in 1952, and President Johnson and the Democrats in 1968. They also had a tsunami effect on Democratic elected officials. In both election years, the Democrats had a decisive edge over the Republicans in Congress, a wide body of public support, and political prestige. Eisenhower, and later Nixon, painted Korea and Vietnam as a hopeless muddle that Truman and Humphrey (in tandem with Johnson) made a mess of. The two Democratic presidents paid dearly for it, and Bush and the Republicans paid just as dearly for the Iraq muddle.

Vietnam has been a dread for presidents. It also implanted another lesson, a lesson that W. Bush took to heart in Iraq, and Obama was repeating in Afghanistan. The lesson is that the way to win wars is not solely to provide maximum firepower and material support to the troops, but also to have a firm political will to not cut and run when things inevitably go bad.

In an interview in September 2009, Defense Secretary Robert Gates admitted that despite the fact that as he put it "there were too many variables to predict" that preventing the US from setting a firm timetable for victory and withdrawal. Yet, Gates was the picture of iron determination in resolving to stay the course in Afghanistan no matter how long it takes, "We want to give them (the Afghan government) the capacity to protect their own security as well as the security of other nations around the world from threats emanating from Afghanistan."

The operative phrase that the generals repeatedly whispered in the ears of presidents was not to tie our hands behind our backs like the politicians did in Vietnam. This was seen as a sure fire prescription for defeat. Military experts were convinced that the American military was better armed, trained, and physically and mentally conditioned to deal with all types of war scenarios than the rag tag, conscript army of four decades ago.

"I think the United States learned a painful lesson from Vietnam, and that is we bail out, or cut and run, if you will, on people at our peril," noted Frank Gaffney, Center for Security Policy military analyst," As hard as some things appear to be at a given moment, the consequences of doing that particularly over time can be even worse, certainly for the people directly involved, but ultimately I think perhaps for us as well."

Obama knew that history well and believed Afghanistan was the right war and would be fought the right way. He embedded that history into his presidential campaign and continually reminded voters of the history of the Iraq war failure. Financially draining wars take a huge toll on the economy, drag down public morale, and cause a steep plunge in American prestige internationally. It also whips up greater anti-American sentiment.

Three failed and flawed wars and the public's distaste for those wars helped topple two sitting Democratic presidents, and hopelessly discredited a Republican president. The same public distaste for the Afghanistan war could easily make it Obama's Vietnam. The historian at his White House dinner in August 2009, and the history of that war itself served notice on Obama of this grave peril.

CHAPTER 11

Progressives' Obama Quandary

S hortly before congress's annual summer break in August 2009, House Democrats Keith Ellison, John Conyers, and Maxine Waters loudly and defiantly shouted they would not vote for a health care reform bill that didn't include the public option. The three congresspersons are African-American, on the far left side of congress, and at one point Obama's biggest congressional cheerleaders. Their loud grumble and possible threat to defect from backing him on health care was not the isolated pique of staunch friends that suddenly felt betrayed.

60 House Democrats, all members of the Congressional Progressive Caucus, on August 17, 2009 sent Obama a batch of letters warning him that if he scrapped the public option they would think long and hard about voting for the reform bill. The threat was seri-

ous in that it was unlikely that few if any Republicans would back his bill in the House. A defection of 60 Democrats would be more than a political embarrassment it could prove fatal to the bill.

The threat caused enough of a stir in the Oval Office that Obama got on the phone a few days before he delivered his major address on health care before a joint session of Congress and jawboned the leaders of the Progressive Caucus, the Congressional Black Caucus, the Congressional Asian Pacific American Caucus and the Congressional Hispanic Caucus to see whether they really meant business when they said they had deep doubts about backing a bill without the public option.

The opposition to a health care reform deal pointed to a far bigger threat to him than the GOP could ever pose. The threat was the active and passive drift of progressives away from full throated support of his policies.

The brutal reality was that he desperately needed progressives to be the shock troops in Congress and in the field to sell his program and his administration. Red Dog Democrats, bankers, corporate CEOs and lobbyists couldn't and wouldn't do it even though he is the consummate Beltway centrist Democrat. They can't and won't put the passion, energy and most importantly the bodies out there to do the grunt political work to sell his program, and to spearhead Democrats congressional election battles in 2010 and his re-election battle in 2012.

The progressive bodies to do this were there. There were 120 million voters in 2008. The Congressional Black Caucus, the Hispanic Congressional Caucus, and the Congressional Progressive Caucus, the third parties, left leaning labor unions, and left independents together represent an estimated 10 to 15 percent of the overall vote. That's 12 to 15 million voters. However, it's not just the numbers. It's also where the numbers are. The bulk of the voters in Pennsylvania, Ohio, North Carolina and Florida traditionally are Republican, and independent moderate and conservative Democrats. With the exception of Pennsylvania, Bush won these states in 2000 and 2004, and bagged the White House. Obama did not change the voter demographic in these states. He did though drastically rev up the numbers of black, Latino, and youth voters, generally more socially and politically progressive, and those self-designated progressive voters that turned out. This made the crucial difference and cinched his win.

The 2000 election debacle was an instructive guide as to how a small number of bloc votes can tip an election. A significant number of the nearly 100,000 votes that Green Party presidential candidate Ralph Nader got in Florida almost certainly would have gone to Al Gore. This turned a contest that shouldn't have been close into a Bush win or steal. In Ohio in 2004, Bush got 18 percent of the black vote, or nearly 100,000 black votes. In times past, most of these votes would have gone Democratic. If they had in 2004, the vote would have been close enough that Democratic presidential candidate John Kerry almost certainly would have challenged the election result in Ohio.

Progressives within and without Congress screamed at the top of their lungs at Obama to remember the promises he made on health care and that is to back a single payer plan. And even though he backpedaled from that, they implored him to not to back away from the public option; take off the gloves, play hardnosed politics, thumb their nose at the GOP, and shove a real health care reform bill through Congress.

A hard uncompromising fight would do much to reassure distraught progressives that there is still some semblance in him of the progressive Democrat that many thought they were voting for. There was little evidence of that happening during the health care reform battle. Obama's continuing reticence to wage a no-hold barred fight with his opponents did not fit his political approach, style, or philosophy. It was still often the case of stated principle being bumped aside by pragmatic political considerations. He set the pattern for that during the campaign.

He had the standard reservation of liberal Democrats that the stimulus bailout gave too much away to bad behaving, profligate spending banks and Wall Street greed merchants and that massive tax cuts wouldn't do much to help the poor and the middle class unemployed. He backed the bailout and tax cuts, albeit modified, to get the support of a handful of congressional Republicans.

He opposed the Iraq war, but he calculated that if he pushed for a quick and immediate withdrawal the military brass and conservatives would howl and dig in their heels to resist. By the end of his campaign and after his inauguration he talked solely about flexible timetables and a phased withdrawal from Iraq.

In the case of Afghanistan, he sent the strong signal that he'd rush even more troops into the field. This virtually assured that just as Iraq was seen and pilloried as Bush's war and folly, Afghanistan would be seen and pilloried as Obama's war.

The health care retreat and other Obama shifts alone didn't make droves of progressives shut down on him. It was the great fear and expectation that he'd perform more infuriating back flips or do little to expand civil rights, and liberties protections, gay rights, end the wars, and rein in corporations and Wall Street abuses during the next three years of his administration.

This would draw more howls of betrayal and add up to even greater disillusion, despair, and defections among progressives. The defections would be a far greater lethal blow than anything the GOP could deliver.

* * * * *

*T*he one sure way to reassure progressives, and liberal Democrats that they had not done a total back flip on the issues was for him to get down and dirty with the GOP after he was elected on health care and other vital legislative issues. That was not likely to happen. He delivered carefully calibrated rhetorical toss away lines about ending the war, single payer health care, nailing Bush lawbreaking officials, cracking down on the Wall Street greed merchants, and jumpstarting a new war on poverty. Yet he never ceased being a solid team playing Beltway, centrist Democratic and these political positions are anathema to centrist Democrats. To play the centrist political game correctly requires compromise, conciliation, and bipartisanship. Illinois Republicans, and that included some of the most conservative down state Republicans, repeatedly gave Obama high marks as the one upstate Illinois black Democrat who would continually reach across party lines to build consensus to get legislation passed.

He learned early that this was the safe way to bag the big financial and corporate dollars, stay in good stead with the Democratic Party regulars, and garner favorable ink in the mainstream media. He gave

a bigger hint that compromise and conciliation would be the watchwords of his administration in his coming of political age keynote
speech at the Democratic National Convention in 2004. The punch
line that brought swoons and wows was that Americans shouldn't be
pigeonholed into Red States and Blue States and that he would work
hard to close the political and ideological rifts and divisions. This was
a political template for a non-confrontational; don't ruffle the GOP's
political feathers approach to policy matters.

* * * * *

*T*his was totally in keeping with Obama's political bent that
when circumstances dictated he would conciliate moderates
and conservatives on a key issue that might cause political
trouble. This was plainly evident during the presidential campaign
when he and McCain at times sounded more and more like political
Siamese Twins on the issues of expansion of stem-cell research, immigration, faith-based social services, expanded government wiretapping, building more nuclear power plants, global warming, fair
trade, and the death penalty. The similarity between the two was even
more glaring as he edged closer to McCain on his plans on health
care, taxes and the Iraq War. These were supposed to be sacrosanct
Democratic attack points against McCain.

The bitter truth was that he could not have gotten the stamp of
approval from top Democrats, broken the cash registers on fund raising, beat down the Clinton Machine, gotten the parade of endorsements from former Reagan and Bush Sr., and even Bush Jr. officials,
drawn the raves of virtually every major news outlet if there was even

the slightest hint that he would be a "toss caution to the wind", liberal crusader.

He adhered close to the prime dictate of American presidential politics. That is that liberal and moderate Democrats in the early stages of the presidential political game run to the left and move quickly to the center as they sniff the possibility of victory. Republicans do just the opposite. They run to the right and scurry quickly to the center as they get the victory scent.

A big part of Obama's appeal, even mystique, as radically distinct from the political reality of who he is and the interests that he had to represent and conciliate to win, and now govern, was the historic first of being an African-American with a real shot at the White House. The other and probably even greater part of the mystique was the loath of Bush's domestic and war policies, and the public's desperation to rid Washington of him.

In the early going of the presidential campaign, Hillary Clinton was a Clinton, a consummate party insider, wreaked too heavily of the Beltway establishment, and voted to approve and fund the Iraq war. To liberals she represented everything wrong with the Democratic Party.

McCain, Palin, *the Fox News Network*, the gaggle of hard right talk radio hosts relentlessly hammered him as just another tax and spend, big government, pro-minority tilt Democrat. This put Obama on the defensive with conservatives and centrist independents. The upside was that it also cemented his credentials as a liberal reformer who would move Washington politics from the musty, back room special interest wheel and deal good ole boy politics of the past. He said just enough to feed that hope. However, even as he spoke about change, he was careful to keep the door open wide to reshape, massage, and contour policy issues to conform to what was pragmatic, doable and acceptable.

The classic examples were the two biggest issues during the campaign, the war and the economy. Despite the public fury over Congress plopping tens of billions into the pockets of bankers and brokerage houses even before he took the White House, he vigorously backed the Wall Street bailout without pushing for any of the tough regulatory checks on the bankers that liberals and even some conservatives demanded.

Iraq. He dropped all early campaign talk of a speedy troop withdrawal and said that the war would end when the generals and command staff said it would. Neither of these pronouncements tagged him as a play to the gate political backslider. It merely showed that pragmatism in presidential politics is the only real principle that counts when it comes to winning and governing.

* * * * *

Then there was the matter of race. The escalating GOP counterinsurgency against him in the months after his inauguration was fueled by playing on the thinly veiled racial fears of a black liberal leaning president. A president that had allegedly suspect birth, religious ties, and patriotism, and who would subvert the liberties, and economic well-being of law abiding, patriotic hard working white Americans. This was ridiculous, but the scare tactic worked.

A September 2009 survey by the Pew Research Center found a big fall off in his approval ratings. The greatest fall off was among white independents, middle aged voters, and white women. This was just as vital a voting demographic as the votes of progressives. He had bested McCain among them during the campaign. The survey and other polls had even shown that Democrats had inched up on Republicans in getting the blame for the mess in Congress. That made him even more gun shy about trying to ram health care reform, or any other part of his agenda through Congress with Democrats, especially House Democrats, only. This would draw not only howls of dictatorship but stir massive political and public disruption and unrest. This would open the door wide for Republicans to rebound and actually win back a few seats in the 2010 mid term elections. This was a major White House concern. There was good reason. During the president's first midterm election his party has lost an average of 16 seats in every election since 1945.

The specter of a rejuvenated, even more war like GOP was Obama's worst nightmare. The low intensity warfare against him would severely hamper his efforts to better shore up the economy; pass an immigration reform and campaign reform law and wind down the wars. This was not a false fear. South Carolina Senator Jim DeMint who emerged as Obama's most vocal and visible GOP congressional nemesis made that plain in a conference call with an outfit called Conservatives for Patients Rights in July 2009, "If we're able to stop Obama on this. It will be his Waterloo. It will break him." The "this" meant health care reform. The "break him" meant his administration.

The pleading, by progressives and even Bill Clinton at the high point in the health care debate in September, 2009, for him to thumb his nose at the GOP and go it alone with Democrats showed little understanding of who and what Obama was and how he got to the White House. Their plea was political naiveté at its worst, and this was something Obama could never be accused of.

The Year of Crisis and Challenge

I n an interview on *NBC's Today show* in February 2009, two weeks after he was sworn in as president, Obama was frank. He said that if he didn't deliver he'd be "a one term proposition." Obama well knew that he was under the white hot glare of the media, the public and especially GOP attackers to deliver the goods, or be quickly dumped in the presidential has been bin.

The first week he sprinted out the gate. He gathered his top military personnel to talk about Iraq. He promised to close Guantanamo interrogation facility and he demanded daily briefings on the economy. These were grand symbolic gestures. The Iraq war could not be abruptly ended, there were piles of legal issues and problems preventing the abrupt shuttering of Guantanamo, and the economoy would have to work through a long cycle of contraction and realignment before a sustained recovery could be felt. Yet the gestures gave the strong impression that the new administration was on the move. And perception for a young, untested president counted a lot.

Polls backed up the hard political reality that action not gestures was what the public demanded. By mid August 2009 that was glaringly apparent. A *Washington Post-ABC* News survey found that his approval ratings had dived from the off the charts highs he got in the first days in office. Part of the drop could be chalked up to inevitability.

New presidents always ride into office on the crest of both voter hopes and euphoria about the prospect of change and disgust at and voter fatigue with the former seat warmer in the White House. New presidents just as quickly see their approval ratings dip or freefall. It's easy to see why. They try to do too much to soon, promise not to do political business in the old ways, try to make too drastic legislative changes, or quickly reverse the bad old policies of their predecessor. It's the fabled man on the white horse coming to the rescue. This is, of course, just that fable. Real politics and a public craving for immediate action knock that storybook notion for a loop.

Obama gambled that his presidency would be a crowning success if he could beat back the fine tuned, well-oiled, and well-endowed health care industry juggernaut and get a sweeping health care reform plan passed, that's real health care reform, through Congress and into law. Only one president has been able to do that and that was Lyndon Johnson. He arm twisted, browbeat, and out smarted Congress and the health care industry to get Medicare. Obama had neither the activist, prosperous period of the 1960s or Johnson's massive mandate for change going for him.

Above everything else, the voters put Obama in the White House to make the economy right, rein in the Wall Street greed merchants, save jobs and homes, and get the credit pipeline to businesses open. There was dispute, muddle, and political contentiousness to what degree or even whether that could happen in his first year. Instead a raucous, and divisive health care reform fight gave a badly fractured GOP, the butt of scorn and jokes in the aftermath of Obama's election victory, something that it never imagined in its wildest dreams in mid November, 2009 could happen.

This was the wedge to get them back in the political hunt. If anyone had dared say in the early days of Obama's administration that the percent of voters who actually blamed Obama for making a mess of health care reform was in striking range of those that blame the GOP for the mess, they'd have been measured for a straightjacket. But a mid-August, 2009 Pew Research survey found just that. His poll popularity numbers would bounce back and forth throughout the rest of 2009. This showed that Obama's political fate was locked into just how close he came to delivering on his campaign promises, or at least the perception that he came close.

When Congress took its Thanksgiving break in November 2009 the probability was good that Obama would eventually get a health care bill to sign. But it was a bill that dissatisfied as many as it satisfied. Progressives screamed even louder that the bill sans a public option, and deal laden with major pharmaceutical industry giveaways, was smoke and mirrors, a sham reform, and yet another infuriating betrayal of his campaign pledge to change the way business was done on Capitol Hill. The Fox News Network, Limbaugh, and the GOP attackers screamed even louder that the bill and Obama were taking the country down a sink hole. The bill left the majority of voters confused, perplexed, and even more uneasy about the Obama administration's direction, and his oft criticized inability to be the tough, decisive leader that millions took a chance on and backed.

* * * * *

*T*he conventional wisdom was that Obama had plenty of time to get things right. There were two problems with that. One is self-made. Health care and the economy are signature markers for a successful Obama first term, and the justification for a second one. Doubts, unease, or his real or perceived failure make it hard to unhinge that from voter thinking. Blacks, Hispanics, young and progressive voters would still back him no matter what. But the question is would they mount a crusade for other Democrats in the 2010 midterm elections? Equally important, would they turn out in big and impassioned numbers for him in 2012? That wouldn't happen if they felt that Obama waffled or reneged on his key promises. Meanwhile, the GOP would continue to sow more fear, stir the doubts, unease and perceived failures of Obama. The GOP would likely dump its bizarre fascination with Palin, and would have a fat campaign chest, and groom a fresh new GOP face, (just like the Democrats did with Obama).

Yet, a president's popularity ratings in the first year of his administration are virtually meaningless. Reagan's ratings were in the tank mid-way through his first term and he still won a landslide re-election victory in 1984. The real test for a president and how the public rates him is the quality of his leadership. A foreign crisis, a continued souring economy, out of control partisan battles with Congress, fights with major labor and industry groups, and prolonged military adventures are the things that can inflict a mortal wound on a new presidential administration. Every president at some point during their first term has faced a crisis and had to make hard decisions that rankle one group or another.

Apart from the big stuff on the economy, health care, and Iraq, Obama faced two other challenges during the first few months of his administration. They were the Iran meltdown and the rage from gay groups over his backing of the Defense of Marriage Act. But, even if he had done everything right on these issues, something would've cropped up to dip his ratings.

It would be the same during the next three years of his first term. Crisis or no, and no matter how contentious the next batch of issues such as immigration reform, global warming, the continuing fight to right the economy, Supreme Court appointments, and looming troubles with Iran, North Korea, and in the Middle East that would confront Obama, his trademark style and approach to governance wouldn't likely change. That style was stamped with caution, conciliation, give and take, and unwavering devotion to bipartisanship. The clue that he would govern this way that he gave in his presidential candidacy announcement speech in Springfield in February 2007 the first year of his reign remained the strongest evidence of that.

Bibliography

Allen, Mike and Grim, Ryan, "McCain Questions Obama's Radical Ties," *Politico*, April20, 2008

Baker, Peter, "Could Afghanistan be another Vietnam?" *New York Times*, August 23, 2009

Baker, Peter, Bumiller, Elizabeth, "Obama Considers Strategy Shift in Afghan War," *New York Times*, September 23, 2009

Barabak, Mark Z., Anger in the Streets of Washington, *Los Angeles Times*, October 4, 2009

Bedard, Paul, "GOP Strategy: Hit Obama on Spending, Budget, Taxes," *US News & World Report*, September 6, 2009

Brown, Carrie Budoff and Henderson, Nia-Malik, "A Year After Race Speech, Silence," *Politico*, March 18, 2009

Brown, Carrie Budoff, "Liberals Escalate Public Option Push," *Politico*, September 3, 2009

Buchanan, Pat, " Buchanan to Obama: Race—It's a Two Way Street, " *New England Republic*, February 3, 2009

Deen, Mark and Tweed, David, "Banking Problems are now Bigger than Pre Lehman," *Bloomberg Report*, September 13, 2009

Fournier, Ron, "Obama Gambles on Making Nice, No Vetoes," *Associated Press*, September 9, 2009

Heath, Brad, "Poll: 57 % See Stimulus Working," USA Today, August 17, 2009

"Insurers Mount Attack against Health Care reform," *huffingtonpost.com*, October 12, 2009

Isenstadt, Alex, "The Race from Race: Dems Rebut Carter," *Politico*, September 16, 2009

Kennedy, David M., "FDR's Lessons for Obama," *Time*, July 6, 2009

"Liberals Crank up Heat, Send Obama another letter demanding meeting," *the plum line greg sargeant's blog*, September 10, 2009

"Limbaugh, "I Hope Obama Fails, " *thinkprogress.com*, January 20, 2009

Martin, Jonathan, "Democrats see Race Factor for Obama Foes," Politico, September 14, 2009

McManus, Doyle, "Eric Holder's Military Allies," *Los Angeles Times*, October 4, 2009

Nicholas, Peter and Parsons, Christi, "Obama Moves Quickly, Purposefully," *Los Angeles Times*, January 25, 2009

"Obama: No Plans for Additional Troop Increase in Afghanistan," *cnn.com*, September 16, 2009

"Obama says Race not an Issue," *Reuters*, April 27, 2008

Pessin, Al, "Vietnam Anniversary Holds Lessons US Military," *VOA* , April 29, 2005

"Poverty Rate Hits High level," *Reuters*, September 12, 2009

Prins, Naomi, "Obama Tip Toes Around Wall Street's Looming meltdown," *Mother Jones*, September 16, 2009

Przybyla, Heidi, "Socialism Threat has Long History for Health Care Overhaul Foes," *Bloomberg Report*, September 14, 2009

Rich, Frank, "Obama at the Precipice," *New York Times*, September 27, 2009

Saskow, Eli, "The 17 Minutes that Launched a Political Star," *Washington Post*, August 25, 2008

Scott, Janny, "In Illinois Obama Proved Pragmatic and Shrewd," *New York Times*, July 30, 2007

Shapiro, Walter, "For Obama Foes it's the Economy, Not Race," *Politics Daily*, September 17, 2009

Simon, Richard, "Outrage over Joe Wilson's Outburst isn't Dying Down," *Los Angeles Times*, September 11, 2009

Stelter, Brian, "MSNBC Not Shy About Criticizing Obama," *New York Times*, November 15, 2009

"Survey: Direct and Indirect Medical costs for the Uninsured," *North Star News*, September 20, 2009

Thompson, Krissah, "Scholar says arrest will lead him to explore race in criminal justice system," *Washington Post*, July 22, 2009

Vogel, Kenneth P, "Protests Present GOP with Tricky Task, " *Politico*, September 12, 2009

Wallsten, Peter, "Obama Approval Rating drops Among Whites," *Chicago Tribune*, September 16, 2009

Zelized, Julian E, "Did Obama Underestimate His Critics?" *cnn. com*, September 1, 2009

Index